Love Me
or
Leave Me

Contemporary Memoir
Aching Pathways in Relationships

Gurmay Effrige Fraser, MSIE, IMMS, MSW, LCSW

Realprops & Marketing Solutions
Inc/Gurmay E Fraser
Charlotte
North Carolina, USA, 28216
www.gurmayfraser.com
support@gurmayfraser.com
1-980-859-7761
1-704-457-9011

ISBN Paperback: 979-8-9877775-0-3
ISBN eBook: 979-8-9877775-1-0
Library of Congress Control Number: 2023905339

Unless otherwise noted, scriptures are from the Holy Bible:

- King James Version
- New International Version
- New King James Version

Printed in the United States of America

Contents

Acknowledgments ix

Our Relationship 1

Love or Abuse? 12

Being Forced to Settle 20

Escaping My Abuser 24

Hiding within Myself 43

Coming Full Circle 52

Returning to My Abuser 60

The Grace to Endure 76

Lonely in Marriage 85

Married for the Wrong Reason 93

In the Eyes of a Child 101

Spiritual Abuse 110

Healthy vs. Unhealthy Relationships 122

Time to Take Action 131

Putting My Life Together 142

Love Doesn't Hurt 153

Women Matter 158

Prophetic Shape Shifter 167

The Truth about Who We Are 175

Restoration of God's Anointing 182

About the Author 188

Dedication

I dedicate my book, Love Me or Leave Me: A Contemporary Memoir, to my Abba Father, to my beloved Jesus Christ of Nazareth, to the Holy Spirit, and to all the sons and daughters of God as we come into the truth of who God said that we are.

Being Safe in Relationship is Vital

Since God chose you to be the holy people he loves, you must clothe yourselves with tenderhearted mercy, kindness, humility, gentleness, and patience. Make allowance for each other's faults and forgive anyone who offends you. Remember, the Lord forgave you, so you must forgive others. Above all, clothe yourselves with love, which binds us all together in perfect harmony. – **Colossians 3:12-14**

Acknowledgments

I would like to thank God for giving me the idea, inspiration, focus, joy, and strength and for helping me to complete His assignment, *Love Me or Leave Me.*

I would like to thank my children, Deon N. Browne, MSIM, BS, and her husband, Kirkland G. Browne, MBA, BS; and my son, Dawson D. Joseph, PhD, MS, BS, for their love and encouragement and for standing beside me from start to finish. I thank my children for allowing me to share my passion and for me to become the voice for the voiceless to "change minds and heal nations."

Thank you so much to my friends and fans for reading and reviewing my book, *Love Me or Leave Me*, and for sharing your excitement and your anticipation to see and feel *Love Me or Leave Me* in your hands.

<h1 style="text-align:center">Endorsement by</h1>

Deon Natisha Browne

Love Me or Leave Me: A Contemporary Memoir begins during a time when domestic violence has reached a crescendo. The reader is quickly pulled into the book with a tense scene of domestic violence with insights and wisdom related to abuse—why it happens and what we can learn spiritually from the fact of abuse itself and how to overcome it.

We never know what people are going through. But this book, *Love Me or Leave Me,* was made to help people get out of situations that have held them hostage. To God be the glory!

By Ron Holland, author of *The Fire in My Words: The Anthology of a Social Provocateur*

Love Me or Leave Me: Contemporary Memoir written by Gurmay Fraser is a daring and fascinating look into the harrowing impact of domestic violence. Readers of *Love Me or Leave Me* will have a difficult time escaping the haunting images of abuse Fraser weaves throughout the book. The physical and verbal assaults employed by the character/monster Bert are a deeply disturbing affront to loving relationships.

By Karen Parker | President & CEO

I liked the way you talked about abuse vs. love in *Love Me or Leave Me: A Contemporary Memoir* and discussed the challenges around defining abuse. Your illustration will help the readers to more closely examine their own relationships and offers a guide for acknowledging and taking steps to break free from an unhealthy relationship. I also really appreciated how you talked about witnessing abuse in your family. I think witnessing abuse often causes people to normalize violence later in their own relationships, and it's important that you called this out!

Nakesha Dawson

I found the book *Love Me or Leave Me: A Contemporary Memoir* an intriguing story for people who are married, single, or "complicated." I found myself reading and thinking, "I know this person" or "I've heard of this situation." I found the story real, and I could hear the narrator's voice like she was my friend.

By Myra Patterson-Stewart, M.Div., CEO & Founder
The Deborah Company International

Love Me or Leave Me: A Contemporary Memoir was really good. It exposed spiritual abuse in several different areas of our lives, from women to the pulpit from several different angles. It was enlightening and made me want to read more. It is so about knowing who we are and valuing ourselves. Knowing our self-worth is so important! And when we learn to love ourselves, these behaviors will be unacceptable to us. Another great point is that we must keep our hearts and eyes focused on God that we might not be led astray and into any type of abusive relationship, but most important is that one leaves when this occurs. God blesses!

Our Relationship

Bert and his family live in Georgetown, Guyana, South America, in the city. Bert's father and mother were not married. Bert has three siblings: an older brother and sister and a younger sister. Bert's younger sister was married and gave birth to a son and daughter for her husband. This sister suffered many years in the marriage due to her husband's infidelity for many years. She suffered from many mental health diagnoses, including depression, and she eventually committed suicide. Bert's oldest sister was married with a son and daughter for her husband. He was a lightweight boxer as well as employed at a pharmacy; she and her husband later divorced. Her ex-husband died shortly after, and her daughter died. Bert's oldest brother remained single and lives a single life. Bert's father died, and his mother is still living with Bert's eldest sister.

Bert is twenty-two years old, weighs 168 pounds, and is six feet and two inches tall. He has wide shoulders and forearms that display healthy and vast muscle mass with a stocky build with fair complexion. He has beautiful curly black hair, beautiful dimples that show his facial expression to be smiling, and he is very handsome with dark brown eyes. He is every girl's dream based on physical appearance.

Bert graduated from high school. He was very good with using his hands to build things, so he joined a company as an apprentice to obtain a trade in construction. He then pursued his trade by attending and graduating from vocational education in the trade and industry field. Bert worked very hard and was recognized for his hard work and mastered his trade in construction, especially building foundations using concrete materials.

Bert enjoyed boxing and pursued his passion by training in the boxing ring as a light heavyweight boxer and enjoyed this sport, especially when he fought his opponents and beat them until they were bloody.

Bert was very social and spent at least five days a week hanging out with his friends after work and talking about current events and women's jobs and responsibilities. He felt strongly about this, and his favorite saying was a woman's place is in the kitchen, and her sole responsibility is to take care of her husband and his needs and their children along with cooking and cleaning. Bert loves action movies, and his best time going to the movies was for the noon matinee at Strand Cinema movie house that charged a reduced rate. His favorite action movie was *Enter the Dragon* starring Bruce Lee. He was passionate about and owned Rolex watches, expensive designer sweaters, and Clark's men shoes. His favorite color was brown. His favorite foods were chicken made many ways, including curried, fried, and stew served with white rice, steamed cabbage, and salad including sliced cucumber. He loved Cadbury chocolate with nuts and hot popcorn from Demico House.

My name is Norah, and me and my family live in Georgetown, Guyana, South America, in Agricola on the East Bank on Second Street in the city. My father and mother were married. I have six siblings: an older sister, a younger sister, and four younger brothers. My sisters were married; my older sister was married two times and had two children, a son and a daughter. My younger sister is divorced with three children. The oldest of my brothers is single; the second brother was never married and has four children, but he was murdered in his home by the police in Georgetown, Guyana. My next brother is married with two daughters, and my youngest brother is single with four children.

I am a young, beautiful fourteen-year-old, a high school tenth grader, weighing 112 pounds and height of five feet and five and a half inches tall. I have gray-green eyes and a huge dark brown afro hairstyle, fair skin, and a small body frame that displays a small waist and long legs. At the end of my school day, I enjoy spending my time doing extracurricular activities: first aid classes, nursing classes, sewing, arts and crafts, taking care of my three youngest siblings, refinishing furniture, baking, cooking, and attending Bible study and prayer meetings at the local church.

I love going to the movies, eating caramel popcorn and fried chicken, going to my friends' homes, and going to the zoo. I met Bert quite unexpectedly as I was hurrying home from school to attend to siblings, chores, and homework.

***

Not again! I can't take another beating. I'm tired of him calling me stupid mother f—— and stupid b——. What pleases him anyway? He's easily irritated. The food is not good enough. He tells me I'm a waste of a wife or a good-for-nothing. If he's angry, he throws the food across the room. For the past weeks, he only speaks to me when he needs to. During the times he does answer, he's abrupt and rude and yells, "What?" Now he's becoming angrier and angrier when his dinner is not ready when he walks through the door. Today his anger penetrates my flesh like a knife slicing an apple because dinner is still not ready; he pushes past me without speaking. Our kids—Angelica, eight years old, and Bert Jr., two years old—are excited to see him, but he ignores them and almost knocks them over. With fisted hands, eyes glaring at me, he runs up the stairs two steps at a time.

His Way or the Highway

Now he's screaming my name, "Norah! Norah!" and demanding I should come up to him at once. I can hear him hitting the wall, and he screams louder and louder, "Norah, Norah!" I am preparing our kids for dinner. He doesn't help with anything around the house— no dishes, no cleaning, no cooking, and neither does he pick up after himself. He leaves his dirty dishes at the table and his dirty clothes on the floor. He tells me a wife's job is to pick up and clean up after her husband because she is his helper. He says his father did not clean, and his mother did everything in the house. He says a good wife does not work, but caters to her husband's and children's every need.

Bert becomes agitated when the table is not set and his food is not ready to be served when he walks through the door, like today. Bert does not sit with our daughter Angelica, or notice how she's doing, or review her homework, or put her to bed. Bert does not read to either of our children. Bert calls it a waste of time to take our kids to the park or to engage them in any community activities. He says his parents did not read to him or involve him in any community activities. Bert says it's a waste of time to go to church, and he's not giving any pastor his hard-earned money, and he better not find out I'm giving money to any church either. Bert hates my job and is trying to get me fired again. Some of my previous bosses fired me when Bert visited these jobs and threatened the employees because they refused to answer his calls. He curses my bosses when they redirect him. At my previous job, he disrupted and terrorized my coworkers. My boss let me go because she feared Bert would harm her. Bert inflicts fear in everyone when he is angry.

Answer Your Call

He's screaming, "B———, come here now!"

I ignore Bert, and I'm washing the pots that was used to cook breakfast and dinner today and running the dishwasher to avoid his screams. I'm afraid to answer his call, let alone go upstairs to see what he wants. I can't take another beating from him. It's bad enough he tells me how stupid I am and what a useless wife I am. Bert tries his hardest to strip me of my self-esteem, self-worth, and confidence by terrorizing me and calling me weak and crazy, and he plays all kinds of mind games. He leaves or removes things from their places and swears he didn't do it, and then yells at me, convincing me I did it. But tonight, Bert will not deplete my energy. I will not argue or listen to him screaming, telling me how stupid I am. My body is still not healed from his last assault because Bert's dinner was not ready.

Attack of the Vessel

Tonight, the dinner is not ready when Bert comes home. He yells and screams my name. "Norah!" He demands to know why his dinner was not ready. I start to answer him when Bert punches me in my mouth, one tooth flying and blood gushing. Another tooth is loose, and the force of his blow cuts my lips and fractures my lower jaw. My face is swollen like a small watermelon. Blood gushes from my jaw and mixes with the blood from my lips, spewing all over the floor. I am enraged but react in a way that will not provoke him for fear of more beatings. I try to run from his reach, which makes him angrier. I slip on my blood and fall, and he catches me by my hair and wraps it around his big hands and yanks it so hard while pulling me toward him.

He continues to pull my hair and watches me with hatred in his eyes as I keel over, screaming in pain, pleading with him to let me go. He lets go of my hair, but shoves me into the furniture. He rushes over and continues to kick me with his construction boots, while he uses his fist to punch me all over my body. The force of the punches sends me crashing into the wall, and I collapse on the floor while he continues to kick me.

I don't know how long I lie on the floor. I fall asleep and continue to drift in and out of sleep. As I wake up, I taste a salty liquid in my mouth, and I struggle to open my eyes. I begin to fight to sit up, but keep slipping until I muster enough strength to wiggle away from the pool of blood on the floor. I use the wall for support to stand.

When I look in the mirror, my face and eyes are swollen beyond recognition. It takes me some time to process the full details of what happened, and the more I process, the more I become afraid of Bert.

The reality of my situation crushes me with fear because I don't know what Bert will do next, but I can see now what he is capable of doing.

The house phone rings, and I answer it. Bert talks to me through the phone, saying that I made him do what he did, and if I want to see our kids again, I better not seek medical help or say anything to anyone. I am petrified and beg Bert to bring my babies home. I promise not to seek medical help or to say anything to anyone. Bert demands that I quit my job, and I agree.

An hour later, Bert brings the kids back home, but does not allow them to see me, insisting I stay in my room. My kids and I talk for a short time through my locked bedroom door. Angelica and Bert Junior want to see me, but I tell them they can't. They cry and bang on the door, and Bert yells at them and threatens to spank them. This makes them cry even harder, and I can hear him spanking them as he drags them away from my door. I spend most of the night crying in severe pain. Bert attempts to administer first aid by cleaning the cuts and bruises all over my body, saying all the while, "See what you made me do."

Healing Process

My physical wounds take several months to heal with severe pain and swelling throughout my body. I have problems sleeping, eating, and speaking. My skin changes colors, and I am embarrassed for anyone to see me like this, especially my children. My face is now healing, and the black-and-blue marks fade into purple. I can still feel the pain, and I can still see the swollen hair follicles left where Bert yanked and held my hair. This traumatizes me and reminds me to always listen to him. But this also angers me. I can't stand Bert touching me, but I'm afraid to tell him no.

I plan how to leave him while I still can, but I can't even leave the house now because of the pain, bruises, swelling, and discoloration. Bert is happy to report to my job that I will not be returning.

He keeps the kids home from school and takes time off from his job to watch me to make sure I keep my word and don't report the beating to anyone. Bert drills me repeatedly about how I should respond if anyone comes to the house or if I should be asked what happened to my face or skin. My jaw stays in a bandage while I can't speak well. My meals are an all-liquid diet, and I drink with a straw, but swallowing is painful. Sitting too long is stressful on my body, and I use a heating pad in areas that are still badly bruised. I dream of leaving this pain forever when Bert's screams bring me back to the reality at hand.

Still No Answer

Bert is yelling, "Norah, why the hell are you not answering me?"

Bert continues to scream my name. "Norah! You b———! Where the hell are you?"

My mouth is dry. My hands are clammy, and I begin to shake. I can feel the perspiration dripping down my back. I try to find the right words to say to him, but none come. My mouth opens and shuts. My god, what should I say? Panic and fear grip my body. I can feel some kind of altercation rising between us from the tone in his voice. It's inescapable. I am afraid to answer and afraid not to answer. I feel any answer would be wrong. Is Bert going to attack me like he did two months ago? My god, what is going to happen this time? When will this nightmare end? Maybe this time he will not assault me—he did promise last time he would never raise his fist or his boots on me ever again.

Any Answer Is Wrong

Any answer is wrong when Bert is angry. If I answer him in a manner he finds unacceptable, he hits me in the mouth, and when I don't answer him at all because of fear, he attacks me by hitting me with his fist and kicking me with his boots.

I decide to answer him. "Bert, I'm busy setting the table for dinner. Please come down so we can eat."

Bert walks to the top of the stairs. "B———, come upstairs now. You're making me angry."

I reply, "I can't—it's dinnertime."

Bert is quiet for a moment. I have refused to give in to his demands. I have disobeyed him. He remains upstairs and silent. I proceed to serve my children dinner and eat. Still silence upstairs. We finish eating, and I clean the rest of the dishes, counters, and kitchen floor. Maybe he will let this fight go. I check Angelica's homework. All the while, now Bert remains upstairs without making a sound.

But now Bert is stomping down the stairs, yelling, "Where the hell are you, Norah? What did I tell you about disrespecting me in front of our children? B———, when I call you, you must come right away. Now you deserve what you get."

His steps quicken as he stomps down the stairs screaming, cursing, and yelling. "Stupid mother f———, where the hell are you?"

Out of Harm's Way

I must not let our kids see him assault me again. I can feel his anger like the force of a volcano coming toward me. I freeze in place and tremble. My kids hold on to me and refuse to leave. Bert grabs the kids and throws them across the room. They scream. In my panic, I try to escape from Bert and run toward our children, but Bert charges toward me. I yell, "Kids! Hurry upstairs to Angelica's room and stay there!"

Angelica grabs Bert Junior's hand, and they dash upstairs, screaming all the way. I hear the bedroom door slam shut.

Human Punching Bag

I hear a rushing sound as Bert charges toward me, and he throws combination punches that land on my head, face, and other parts of my body. The last thing I remember is being hurled across the living room, hitting the wall, and collapsing on the floor. While lying there helpless, Bert kicks my hands, legs, stomach, and face. Drifting into and out of consciousness, he continues punching and kicking and calling me a stupid mother f——, shouting, "This is what you get for disobeying me!"

It feels like an eternity passes when I rouse and feel severe, sharp, shooting pain throughout my body while tasting salty liquid on my lips and clamminess on my body. I no longer hear Bert's voice or feel his kicks. I don't know if I fall back into a doze, but when I wake up again, I can hear my children's voices crying and screaming. "Mommy, please wake up!"

Saved by My Guardian Angels

When God said He would give His angels charge over me, it was true. I hear the voices of my two angels, eight-year-old Angelica and two-year-old Bert Junior, sobbing in between screams. "Mommy, wake up!"

I feel little hands pulling and tugging my body and wiping the blood from my face. I begin to sit, and my head feels heavy. Warm liquid is all over my face. My eyelids are heavy as I struggle to open my eyes. Blood is all over the floor and still dripping from the cuts on my body. Suddenly, flashbacks of the evening replay in my head, and I see furniture destroyed and tossed around me. I try getting up, but pain overwhelms me. I fall back on the floor, but with the help of my children and support of the wall, I am able to get up to sit on a nearby chair.

Where Do I Go from Here?

Why don't I leave him? How do I leave him? I want my children to be raised by their father. So many questions and no answers, and I don't know where to begin. Maybe if I obey Bert, he will change. He experienced hard times growing up. His parents were mean to him. His father beat him and his mother, and sometimes they were locked out of their house. Bert is not always mean. If I leave him, who will care for him? I can't tell anyone about what's going on in my house or relationship with Bert. My family and friends would not understand. His behavior is good when his mood is.

But what if Bert does not change? Suppose something bad happens to my children, like they get hurt when Bert is assaulting me? Or what if he hurts me? What would happen to my children? I'm not only endangering my life, but also my children's lives. I need help, but who can I trust? Bert's physical and emotional abuse is out of control. His frequent horrifying physical assaults and the chronic cloud of imminent danger paralyzes me. I make excuses for Bert's abusive behaviors. I lie and cover up his physical and sexual assaults. I lie to my family, friends, coworkers, and doctor about how I get the bruises on my body. His behavior is worse now, and when he gets in a rage, I don't know the person he becomes. I am numb with fear, which is intensifying daily and lasting longer now. I'm beginning to think something terrible may happen to my children and me. I must forgo his lies, the promises he made to me but never kept.

Over the years, things have become worse between Bert and me, and the rages are intensifying.

I sit on the chair and pray to God. *What should I do? What is right? God, I need Your help. This is Norah, Your daughter.*

Love or Abuse?

I met Bert at age fourteen. On my way home from school, Bert appeared behind me, saying, "Hi, Reds."

I turned around to gaze into a pair of big dark brown eyes. Here was quite a handsome male, about six feet two inches, with the most beautiful olive skin, curly black hair, with a well-built six-pack, in his early twenties, riding a bike behind me. He introduced himself as Bert, and I introduced myself as Norah.

He said, "Your beautiful gray-green eyes are new to me." I blushed.

Bert said, "Wow, you are beautiful. I'm sure you're used to such compliments."

I pretended not to hear him.

He said, "I watch you go by, but today, I am introducing myself to you." Bert continued to stare at me as he rode his bike beside me. I walked ahead of him because I was uncomfortable, and he continued to stare at me. Feelings of uneasiness overpowered me, so I walked as fast as I could away from him.

Bert caught up with me and asked, "Are you trying to avoid me?" He laughed, and I could see perfect dimples with beautiful level-white teeth. It was so hot and sunny that perspiration soaked my blouse, and I could feel it running down my back. I was so embarrassed because I could feel my blouse sticking to my body. I tried not to draw attention to myself by pulling it to fix it. If I ever felt like running home, it was in that moment. I felt the perspiration spread across my body as the hot sun continued to burn my face and arms.

Stranger in My Midst

Why is this stranger interrupting my peace? I wondered. *What does he want, and why is he speaking to me?*

I guess Bert sensed my discomfort and switched the conversation. He began to ask me about people in my community and wanted to know if I knew his friends and family. I refused to answer and avoided his gaze. He asked me about students who attended my school. This did not make me feel any better, and I hoped he would leave me alone and disappear with the same speed he appeared. His probing made me uncomfortable.

Bert turned to look at my face and said, "Why are you so quiet?" I could hear my heart pounding through my blouse and felt the perspiration moving down my back even more. He now pushed his bike as he walked so close to me, I could smell the fragrance of his cologne, which made me feel light-headed. Bert was in my space, making me uncomfortable. I was annoyed because he invaded my privacy. I mustered my courage and asked him to leave, but he ignored me and continued to probe. I felt even more frustrated and uneasy. I said, "Bert, I don't entertain discussions from strangers."

He grinned and said, "My friends warned you play hard to get." After several attempts to engage me, he gave up. He whispered, "I'm patient and will be back." He grinned and winked at me as he rode off, turning his head to glance back at me.

I shifted my gaze from him to prevent him from seeing me staring at him. After this encounter, he continued to pop up, but I refused to acknowledge his presence. I changed my route to avoid him, but he found my new route. My peers considered me the most unpopular teenager in school. I came close to failing miserably in all my classes.

Many of the students turned their noses up as they walked past me and muttered words like *stupid, ugly,* and *dummy.* Bert told me how beautiful I was and continued to show me attention. My peers began to whisper and murmur about Bert's undivided attention toward me. They asked questions about Bert's attraction to me. How did the most handsome young man get stuck on me? These students debated and voted me as the least likely to make it, "the ugly duckling."

Sent by God or the Defeated Devil?

When God wants to bless you, He sends His blessings through a person. When the defeated devil wants to destroy you, he sends his destruction through a person. Who's in your life, and who sent him? Whom are you taking council from? We need to keep close tabs on our enemies, but we should keep closer tabs on our friends. Our enemies stay away from us, but people we call friends know our secrets and want our resources without the price or sacrifice. Has your life changed since this person entered it?

God provided us with many Bible stories for us to receive revelations and wisdom. We ignore these warnings because we don't understand how the Bible is connected to our daily walk with our Creator, God. Remember, Joseph's brothers put him in the pit and sold him into slavery because of their jealousy. God revealed visions and dreams to Joseph, and he shared them with his family. Instead of celebrating this, they turned against Joseph. Like Jacob, who wanted the blessings of the firstborn anointing that belonged to his brother Esau. Jacob masterminded a scheme with his mother to get the blessings his father Isaac wanted for Esau. And then there's Cain and Abel. Cain killed Abel, his brother, because Abel brought an acceptable first fruit blessing to God, and God blessed Abel. Again, jealousy propelled a hateful crime. Some people follow the devil's lead.

Many times we feel we can't do something we know we should. When we understand that we are able to do difficult things through God, all things are possible. But we must seek God first instead of people. Many times people in leadership abuse their authority at jobs, homes, and churches. Even King David took Bathsheba, had sex with her, and later arranged the death of her husband, Uriah. But God is also a god of war. We must be careful whom we take counsel from and for what purpose before we give them titles and assignments they didn't earn or don't deserve.

My peers never appreciated me, and I suspected they didn't like me. Some of them changed their behavior toward me when Bert showed me attention, and they wanted to know my secret for attracting him. They wanted Bert's attention and would stop at nothing to get it, presenting him with personal gifts to entice him. Because Bert gave me lots of attention, some of my peers only became my friend to learn what they thought was my secret power. Enticed by this attention from my peers, I allowed Bert to show me off to his friends. My peers accepted and included me in their circle.

Bert wanted to know how I felt about him. At fifteen years old, Bert began to pressure me to date him. In my culture, dating meant talking and going places, like art shows, picnics, movies, dances, and concerts. I delayed confirming our dating until Bert threatened to date my peers. I did not like this idea because I would become the laughingstock and be teased again by these peers.

Fear caused me to agree to Bert's demands, and he showered me with expensive gold and diamond jewelry. He made a lot of money and bought me things I did not want, such as clothes. Some of these clothes were custom-made. I refused his gifts and money on many occasions. Bert became upset, but I continued to refuse his money. I remained reserved with Bert, trying to keep boundaries between us. I refused any emotional attachment to him. When his behavior made me uncomfortable and I tried to return his jewelry, he was displeased. He said if I didn't wear the jewelry, his friends would call him cheap and taunt him. Feeling sympathy for him, I wore his expensive jewelry.

Bert wanted marriage, and I refused. He became angry and tried to convince me that marrying him and moving away was a great plan. I witnessed his anger and his controlling behaviors as I shared my plans with him, which didn't align with his dreams. We argued about our relationship, in particular his desire for marriage. Bert dictated whom I should speak with or be friends with. He wanted to approve where I went, how long I stayed, and he wanted to know every detail about my time. He did not trust me around some people because he felt they would influence me. I refused to listen to him and continued going places with new friends. We disagreed about many things, and we were both frustrated. I enrolled in many extracurricular activities to avoid him. But of course, this only caused further disagreements, so I no longer shared my activities with him or my plans. I became tired of our fights. He threatened to date the young women in my community. Again, I panicked when he threatened this because I knew my peers would reject and tease me. His threats worked, and I gave in to his demands.

But Bert only became more and more demanding, and this caused us to argue more and more. I grew so tired of our arguments because he ignored my wishes, claiming that my displeasure would only display to others that we disagreed and make us a source of ridicule. His behavior embarrassed me, so I gave in to what he wanted. After I agreed with Bert that we should not publicly argue, he intensified his demands that he approves of my whereabouts and with whom I should go places. Imagine me, Norah, who had no intention to be talking to or making any commitment while in high school now finds myself getting deeper in a relationship that could lead me into lots of problems. I wanted peace with him; therefore, I lied and called him my knight in shining armor. I convinced myself he came to save me from my cruel peers.

Who Sent Him?

My energy level continued to be depleted while keeping up with Bert's demands because he required so much attention. It became all about him. Besides his job and me, nothing else was important to him. He chose not to develop his personal life. Bert depleted my joy and my focus and wanted to control my activities and my whereabouts. I didn't like this at all.

He told me he never wanted to be away from me. Bert wanted a detailed report for every hour I spent away from him. He told me he loves me, and I'm a lucky girl. He said he chose me over all the girls, and those girls are jealous. He told me he loves and misses me and can't live his life without me.

Bert wanted more than what I could offer. I refused, and he began to harass me. His behavior mentally and spiritually drained me. My church attendance and reading of the Bible became limited because he always wanted us to be together. My God, who did I get myself involved with? Who sent him? All Bert talked about was getting married as soon as I turned seventeen and leaving our city and moving far away from our family and friends.

How Could This Be Love?

I graduated high school and became involved in community and volunteer programs several days a week to avoid him. Seeing Bert daily frightened me. His expectations increased to seeing me each morning, lunchtime, and in the late afternoon. Bert said he expected me to be home more and available when he showed up. I would disappear with friends or my cousins to the movies and neglected to inform Bert. When he would come by expecting me to be home, my whereabouts would be unknown to my family because I did not want anyone to share this information with Bert. However, when Bert and I reconnected, he would be angry, use profanity, and clench his fists, sometimes punching the walls or throwing things. I would move to prevent being hit. His eyes would be glaring and wild. During those times, I did not recognize him.

He made me afraid and insecure. His new thing would be to curse, scream, and call me all sorts of negative names. Sometimes when he asked me a question, if my response was not pleasing to him, he called me "stupid" and would demand I repeat the answers he wanted to hear. He held grudges for a long time and would remind me of what I did to him and how I made him mad. He never apologized, but would demand an apology from me. He would often be tense with his hands fisted.

He would criticize any person I would be seen with. Bert found something wrong with anyone he saw or heard me speaking with. Bert wanted me all to himself. Bert learned to use manipulative tactics to control me as he applied his charm to influence my family, friends, and people around us, and he studied my culture and traditions as ways to connect with my family. Bert became nice to my family and would volunteer to do favors for them at no cost. My family began to say what a great guy he was and welcomed him into the family.

We would disagree over stupid things, such as me wanting to spend time with my family and friends or me taking classes to enhance my skill sets. When I disagreed with him, he would belittle me. I began to feel my self-esteem crumbling, and I would give in to him to avoid the embarrassment of his unpredictable outbursts.

Over time, Bert began to gain so much control over me. Bert would convince me I provoked these situations and deserved the way he treated me. He went on to say he was not treating me any different from how my aunts' and cousins' husbands treated them. Bert convinced me that if I listened to him the first time and didn't disagree, he would not lose his temper. Nor would he curse or call me derogatory names, punch me, or throw things at me. I made a decision to stop dating him.

My Peers Share Their Experiences

Girls my age and older women would talk about how their boyfriends or husbands curse them and beat them up. Some girls shared with me that their husbands use profanity and call them all kinds of derogatory names and that this is their way of showing love. Now I see these same girls with all kinds of bruises on their bodies. Some girls had to go to the hospital for broken body parts, burns, or injuries. These girls used to talk about loving their men, and now I see sadness and bitterness in their eyes. They no longer laugh and talk about the wonderful things they do with their men, as before these women would share stories about fine dining and wonderful gifts and relationships that once brought happiness. Other girls agreed that their husbands abusing them meant that their husbands loved them.

Being Forced to Settle

Bert talked about our marriage, of me marrying him on my seventeenth birthday. He opposed me spending time with anyone besides him. He complained when I went places with my family or friends. He wanted me home while he worked. Once I discouraged Bert visiting me because I had church activities, but an emergency happened that prevented me from going to church. A gossiper told Bert he saw me speaking to a young man for hours. Bert got angry and accused me of lying and having an affair with this guy. Bert yelled and balled his hands into fists as he punched walls while shouting, "You're a liar!"

I got angry at his accusations.

He said, "When the cat's away, the mice will play." He was convinced I had flirted with this man behind his back. Bert hurt my feelings with his abusive behavior. I took off his jewelry and threw them at him. I ran from my home, leaving him to deal with his emotional upheaval. I returned home when I knew he would be gone. He wrote a letter to me stating that he did not like me speaking to any guy and that I am stupid. He left the jewelry with the letter and said he bought them for me and will not take them back. As was typical, there was no apology in the letter.

Two weeks went by before he showed up at my home. Not only did he not apologize for his behaviors, he told me that he did not forgive me for mine. Instead, he went to the friend I was speaking to that day and threatened him for speaking with me. Our relationship became traumatic, but I didn't visualize things would evolve the way they did.

Being Stalked

My next episode with Bert happened while at a classmate's home. We chatted when she changed the conversation and asked, "Did you come with someone?" "No," I said.

"A man on a bike pulled up when you did, and look—he's still there waiting," she said.

I looked and saw Bert sitting on his bike, waiting. Fear of the unexpected with Bert caused me not to leave until he left. Later, Bert visited my home and accused me of cheating on him. He said he followed me and saw me go into a man's house. "Something is wrong with you, Norah. You don't recognize my value, so now I will entertain the women who want me!" he screamed.

"Go ahead with whatsoever pleases you, but I will socialize with whom I choose," I said. He made me so unhappy. I shared my feelings with him, but he ignored them. I felt uneasiness in my spirit and wanted to let go of our relationship before he abused me.

Flashbacks of Abuse or Love

Bert's offensive behaviors reminded me of the actions I witnessed women in my family and community sustain from their husbands and boyfriends. I refused to allow Bert to abuse me anymore, so I advised him we would need to put some space between us in our relationship. Bert made it clear he couldn't tolerate not seeing me. He went on to say he couldn't imagine me being with anyone else in any relationship or seeing me socializing with anyone else. Bert's eyes were wild. He made a fist and punched the wall, saying, "They would give you bad advice. I don't approve of your friends. A relationship with any of them is not an option!"

His words got my attention because I was worried about his temperament, mood, and attitude. His stance confirmed my fear about him. How can he say he loves me, but belittle me and think nothing about my feelings? How can Bert take our relationship for granted and behave like a slave master? These are signs of abuse.

Abuse or Love?

He clenched his fists and threw objects at me. I ran to prevent being hit. Looking at him, his eyes would glare like a raving lunatic. I was petrified to be alone with him when he was angry. He cursed, screamed, and called me all sorts of names. He reminded me that this was my fault—what I did to him made him this livid. He never apologized, but would demand an apology from me. He continued to criticize and find something wrong with anyone he saw me with.

Violence in My Family Concealed as Love

I witnessed abuse done to women in my family and in my neighborhood. My biological father smacked my mother once, and she tossed a pot of hot rice on him. He ran so fast while screaming as the hot rice burned him. He never hit my mother again. I witnessed my own family members beaten with deadly weapons. I always wondered why they stayed in these abusive relationships. I visited my cousin once when her husband came home intoxicated. He asked for his dinner, but it was not ready. He cursed her then punched her in the mouth. She staggered backward while blood dripped from her mouth. He said, "You are a stupid, no-good wife that I should never have married."

I told him never to hit my cousin or call her names. He called me a "nigger" and yelled that I should never visit his house again. He charged toward her and struck her in the left eye. The force of the blow thrust her backward, throwing her into the living room table as blood gushed from her face and eyes. She keeled onto the table and lay motionless for what seemed to be an eternity. I screamed along with her children. I rushed toward her, and after much pulling and tugging and screaming, she opened her eyes. Her left eye swelled beyond its normal size, and she couldn't see. She had no usage of her left eye. Her husband said she caused it. She cried, and I cried as I witnessed this shocking experience.

Escaping My Abuser

I had to be discreet because I feared Bert would harm me if he knew I was leaving. If I wanted change, I had to be the change agent. From what I had seen, things will only get worse with Bert. I chose not to stay before something bad happened to me.

Bolting from Bert

He had become so jealous, and I needed his permission to do the things I enjoy. My energy, motivation, desires, excitement, time, and creativity had diminished. He was now pressuring me to get physical with him. He said, "Show me, Norah, how much you love me."

I said, "I only want to be friends with you."

Bert said, "I want more with you. My friends told me the only reason you're holding out is because you're cheating."

"Believe what you want," I spat, "but I choose not to become physical with you."

Bert said if he couldn't get me, no one else would.

I said, "I don't care about what your friends are saying. I don't want to be friends with you anymore. You make me feel unsafe."

Whenever I would voice my opinion, it made him angry. When he would ask me what my thoughts were, and I would express myself honestly, he would become irate. He would place his fingers on my face and push his shoulders into me. He blamed me when something went wrong in his life. He never apologized and showed no remorse. He took an interest in tormenting me, and I would always apologize. He reminded me of everything I did wrong. He criticized me for allowing my friends and family to give me advice against his wishes.

Bert became unbearable. I did not even want to speak with him. I told him I didn't want to be friends with him any longer. He tried to persuade me that I needed him to protect me. I decided to get away from Bert before things become unsafe for me. I couldn't share my feelings with anyone for fear Bert would find out. Bert brainwashed my friends and some of my family. I got an invitation for a vacation, and I accepted it to disappear from Bert. I came up with an exit plan to leave Bert to get my freedom back to do the things I enjoy.

Timing Is Important When Leaving Your Abuser

I had to get away. On my departure date, Bert entered my home and stole my packed suitcase. How did he know my plan to travel, I had no idea. Only one of my family members knew when I planned to leave. In my fury, I grabbed other clothing and tossed them into a bag and sprinted to board the city bus to the ship. I got to the ship, met my aunt, and ran to our cabin and locked myself in, for fear Bert would find me and kidnap me off the ship. I did not trust his judgment, and I feared him.

Looking out my cabin window, I saw Bert board the ship. He rushed toward my window as he swung my suitcase in his hand. He begged me to come out for a talk. I refused and reminded him that I had chosen to not speak to him. He continued to talk, and I moved from the window while pulling the blind down.

The captain blew the whistle for visitors to leave the ship in preparation for departure. Relieved, peace came over me for the first time in a long while. I waited until the ship set sail before I found the courage to leave the cabin.

Crossing Paths with Love

Stepping outside my cabin, I saw this handsome man looking up at me, and I felt electricity race through my body. He smiled and said, "I'm Aubrey." This is how Aubrey and I met, and we started a conversation about the weather and our journey and expectations for the trip. Aubrey was 6'2" in height, weighing about 175 pounds, dark, very handsome, short crew cut hairstyle, slim, and very muscular. Aubrey was fashionably dressed in a white T-shirt and a pair of jeans. Aubrey mentioned that he was an only child. He was travelling to Matthews Ridge in the northwest region in the country to work with the Guyana National Service. He's a sergeant of a squad, and this is his first assignment in that region. Of course, I didn't tell Aubrey everything about my trip. Our conversation continued with things we liked and what excited us. Aubrey shared with me that he overheard Bert's plea to talk about our relationship. Aubrey asked, "Why are you scared to leave the cabin?"

I said, "I am running away from him because he frightens me." I began to share how Bert had inflicted such fear in me by losing his temper, throwing and hitting things when he disagreed with my decisions, controlling what I do, where I go, and who I'm with, and calling me names. I told Aubrey how I had become so intimidated with Bert's behavior and reactions that I felt it would only be a matter of time before he began to abuse me. Bert used profanity when speaking to me whenever I did anything he did not give me permission to do. Bert would become explosive and push me and knock me down.

Aubrey and I talked all night and the following day about life, family, education, travel, and about things that excite us. Speaking with Aubrey gave me hope and reassurance. I felt free as we exchanged ideas and talked about things we are passionate about and speculated about life and plans to achieve goals and to be accomplished in our lives. Aubrey was wise with eloquent speech. I never knew a man could be so caring and understanding and humble. He encouraged me.

Though I knew Aubrey for only a short time, I felt comfortable talking with him. He reassured me, and I felt the trauma and pain dispersing from my spirit, replaced with a high level of confidence and peace unlike anything I felt with Bert. Aubrey and I formed a bond during our trip, and we became inseparable. We began to imagine how our lives would connect as we compared our individual plans and what this would mean for each of us. We discussed things we liked and what we didn't like. We shared our food and drinks and laughed at each other's jokes.

Our trip together ended when the ship anchored in Morawhanna. Aubrey's company sent a special speedboat to get him and his crew. Aubrey had difficulty joining his crew on the boat. He kept leaving them to tell me things he wanted to share with me. We kept hugging and embracing each other and promising to meet within a week. Aubrey whispered he felt so attached to me and wanted this new friendship to continue and would not allow anything or anyone to come between us. Aubrey's crew urged him to get on board so the boat could set sail, and he kept begging for another five minutes until finally his boss came over and reminded him that they must set sail now to connect with the transportation waiting to take them to their housing location. Aubrey and I exchanged our contact information and set a meeting time before he left.

I continued my journey and reached my destination. It was nice to revisit the country after being away for many years. Everything seemed smaller—the houses, streets, stores, and the community. I had no plan for my assignment. I just knew I had to get away from Bert. I suppressed memories of Bert's abusive behaviors toward me and no longer wanted to even think about the fear he inflicted in me.

Thinking about Aubrey reminded me of love and respect. His kind words of encouragement and support helped focus my attention from Bert. Aubrey continued to inform and encourage me daily through his letters. He cared about me and was committed as a friend. He proved to be in a class by himself and demonstrated love and showed me I'm special. Aubrey caught my attention with his kindness and consistency. This was hard for me to forget, and his demonstration of love remained in my heart.

In Love and Being in Love

Aubrey adjusted well to his assignment and responsibility of leading a large number of cadets. His work was demanding, beginning early in the morning and ending in the late afternoons. Aubrey remembered the things I like and don't like. He found time to write me often, and he would tell me about his day and remind me that he was thinking of me. I responded to each of his letters, and we shared our ideas, thoughts, and plans.

Bringing Out the Best in Me

Aubrey brought out the best in me. With Aubrey, I felt I could conquer anything, and this increased my confidence. My performance soared above my expectations, which further enhanced my self-esteem. Aubrey spoke to my potential. He always assured me that the best of me is still waiting to be revealed. Aubrey had eyes only for me. Aubrey never compared me to anyone but myself. Reading his letters reminded me of the words he whispered gently in my ears. None of the men in my family treated their girlfriends or wives special. Instead, they abused their women, and I thought a man was supposed to be harsh. Aubrey showed me another way.

Our First Date

With Aubrey, I felt free in mind, spirit, and body. He had such confidence and wisdom. He was understanding, and the impact he had on me was remarkable. The day for our first date approached. I was filled with excitement and wondered if he would still be as happy to see me as the day we parted.

I awoke early and planned what I would wear and what I would say and how I would react when we reconnected. I dressed for our first date. He came dressed in his service uniform—tall, dark, and handsome. As he saw me, we ran toward each other laughing, my hair flying in the hot sun. We ran right into each other's arms.

Aubrey was more handsome than I remembered. We embraced each other, and both felt the electricity going through our bodies. For a moment, we weren't concerned about anything. How long the embrace lasted, we couldn't tell, but when Aubrey spoke, his voice became tearful. He whispered in my ear how much he longed to see and hold me and how much he missed me and loved me. Aubrey said he never felt this way in his life about anyone. From the last time he saw me until now, he had lots of time to think, and when he thinks about me, it lights up his world. Aubrey told me not one day goes by without him thinking about me. Aubrey told me he keeps my touch, my smile, my words of wisdom, and my beauty in his heart. Aubrey told me he wants us to spend the rest of our lives together. He told me it is difficult to explain how much he loves me.

Our first date on the beach was incredible. He did not want me to do a thing but enjoy myself. He brought the bread, meat, salad, juices, and all the condiments and blankets and toiletries, and we had the most exciting and fun day. We ate and spent lots of time talking, listening to each other, dreaming about the future, laughing, and running on the beach. Aubrey and I enjoyed each other's laughter and tears, and we wished the day would never end. We spent all day on the beach, and as night fell, we looked up at the stars and the moon and began to wish upon each star that we would never have to part. We made a commitment that our relationship would never end. We made a vow to never take each other for granted and to always be true and be here for each other. Before we finally took our separate ways, we made plans to meet at the club Friday night.

New Beginnings

During the second week of August, the temperature rose close to a hundred degrees. Our second date was at the new fabulous nightclub everyone was raving about. My excitement burst as I tried on many different outfits until I found the one that showed off my curves. My cousin was coming to pick me up at 10:00 p.m., and the plan was to meet up with Aubrey at 10:30 p.m. I decided to settle for the silk, off-white, sheer midriff top with a sewed-on inner piece and red stretch miniskirt that showed off my Coca-Cola shape. This I accented with red stiletto shoes and round gold earrings and a pair of bracelets. I finished up my chores for the day and proceeded to get my hair done in the latest Afro hairdo in preparation to be at the club with Aubrey.

As promised, my cousin arrived right on time, and I was dressed, waiting. We traveled to the location to meet Aubrey, who wore the biggest smile. Aubrey was dressed in a tan shirt and beige pants with complementary brown shoes. When Aubrey saw me, he ran toward me, embraced me, and spun me around. He told me how beautiful I looked. I introduced my cousin to him, and we proceeded to the club, walking hand in hand. We danced all night. The music was so good, and the transitions of music from R&B to rockers to reggae kept us on our feet. We laughed, talked, danced, and ate fried chicken and drank soda pops until we left.

Aubrey escorted me home. Parting this time was difficult for both of us. When we said good night, we kept running back to each other and hugging and embracing and telling each other how much we had fun and enjoyed each other's company. We faced each other with tears trickling down the sides of our faces. We did one final embrace and kissed each other on the cheek and said our final good night. I went into the house as Aubrey left to go back to the barracks.

Before Aubrey left, we made arrangements to go on the base at Aubrey's worksite for the grand opening of Papaya National Service. Aubrey promised to provide transportation to and from the base, and we planned to see each other the following week on his day off. We continued to correspond by mail every day. I was excited reading Aubrey's letters. I continued to read different books and explore the countryside. I was invigorated by Aubrey's friendship, and our relationship became an important part of my world. I so much looked forward to seeing Aubrey and sharing and hugging and talking with him. I couldn't wait for the grand opening of Papaya because I would meet Aubrey's colleagues, superiors, subordinates, and cadets for the first time.

I was daydreaming about this happy time when the reality of why I was here in the countryside in the first place came flooding back to me. I continued to imagine what my life would be like with Aubrey, but thoughts of Bert crept into my reveries. When Bert would appear suddenly in my thoughts, I'd go from relaxed to wide awake. It felt like I was being forced to watch a scary movie, unable to run away from the terror.

The Abuser Returns

As I sat on the stairs outside the house, my last confrontation with Bert flashed before my eyes. At that moment, the sun glanced on my face, and I turned to see a bright red object dancing in and reflecting the sunlight. Horror struck me. Bert was walking down the hill toward my family's home, swinging my red suitcase in his right hand. I sat frozen on the stairs, staring at him as he continued to walk toward me. He walked up to me and planted a kiss on my cheek. He said, "Are you shocked to see me? Do you still love me?"

Fear gripped me. Fear of responding and of not responding. I lied and said, "Yes."

He said, "I heard you met a guy on the ship, and the two of you spent hours talking, and you were seen hugging each other when he had to leave to join his crew. You've been seen gallivanting in the community with this man."

I found my voice and courage to ask Bert, "What are you doing here, and how did you know where I am?"

Bert said, "You can't hide from me. Wherever you go, I will find you."

Panic rose within me as Bert pushed past me and proceeded into my family's home. Unknown to me, Bert had made arrangements to stay at my family's home. Inside, he greeted my family, and I heard them all happily discussing his living arrangements as I sat and listened in complete horror.

Under the Same Roof as the Abuser

Bert received permission to stay where I was staying. The details of how Bert knew where I ran to were kept from me. I did not feel safe with Bert around, considering my friendship with Aubrey and us dating and going to events in my community.

Bert joined me on the porch and began accusing me of having an affair with Aubrey. I stared at him in shock, and when I regained my composure, I asked him how he knew where I was and where to find me. He reminded me his spies follow me around and report everything to him. I stood motionless as I stared at him, dumbfounded and speechless. He continued to say that if he couldn't be with me, he wouldn't allow anyone else to be with me either.

I mustered my courage and asked if that was a threat. Bert responded, "You will soon find out."

During the time Bert stayed, he spied on me and followed me wherever I went. I don't know how he knew where I was going. I was silent about my whereabouts, but Bert always showed up. Many times he would sneak up on me. I became terrified of him, especially of the way he would look at me. His demeanor was of anger, and he was always sneering at me. I was afraid of him and afraid to be in the house with him alone. Whenever I went out, I always made sure my cousin walked me into the house. I would leave the house when my family was leaving. When I overslept and woke up to find my family left me alone with Bert, I panicked.

Bert petrified me. He hid in the house and snuck up on me. I would get myself together fast and get out of the house. I asked my family when Bert was planning to leave, but they brushed my question off. Bert was unpredictable and unstable—I had to be careful. I went directly to the postal service to arrange to pick up my mail there and only to have it handed to me with identification. I requested that they never deliver my mail to the house. Daily I would go to the postal service to pick up my mail and to mail my letter to Aubrey. Aubrey's secret agents changed the day and time they met and delivered mail or gifts to me. Aubrey was told about Bert's sudden appearance as well as his tactics and threats to me.

Our Third Date

Aubrey's latest letter detailed our upcoming date's location and time. I gathered my outfit—a stretch black miniskirt with a baby blue satin spaghetti-strap blouse with floral, five-inch Kickers shoes, and colorful accessories of earrings and chain. As usual, my cousin posed as my escort to the club Aubrey and I arranged for our date, and she and I walked to the club. Halfway there, I met Aubrey, and we were so happy to see each other. We ran toward one another, into each other's open embrace. We hugged in pure contentment. We walked hand in hand under the beautiful moonlight. I was pouring out my fears to Aubrey of being around Bert and reported Bert's threats when I saw a male figure standing by the roadside smoking a cigar. It was Bert. I whispered to Aubrey, and Aubrey changed position with me and squeezed my hand, telling me not to be afraid. He said he will protect me.

Bert came out of the shadow and insisted I return to the house with him. I was too afraid to respond, but Aubrey did and introduced himself to Bert and told Bert to leave us alone and that he and I are friends. Bert insisted I was his girlfriend, and Aubrey told him they can set up a time to talk, but this is not the time or place. Bert began to curse, and Aubrey ignored him, and we continued to walk the short distance to the club. Bert went ahead of us and disappeared in the night. Aubrey now placed his hand around my waist and kept whispering, "You are safe. Everything will be fine."

When we got to the club, to my surprise, Bert was standing near the entrance drinking a beer. Bert kept staring at Aubrey and me. Aubrey ignored him and found two seats for my cousin and me and went to get us drinks. A seat became open next to me, and Aubrey sat with us, telling me not to be afraid. Aubrey whispered, "My secret services are with us. I had sent them ahead of us to ensure the place is safe."

I felt better and began to relax. I told Aubrey I was concerned for both him and Bert's safety, and I did not want anything to happen to either of them. Aubrey assured me that nothing bad would happen.

The disc jockey began to play the music Aubrey and I enjoy most, and we got up to dance. At that moment, Bert also got up and rushed toward me and said he will not allow me to dance with anyone but him.

Bert threatened me, saying he would hurt me right there and then if I danced with Aubrey. Aubrey stepped in front of me and warned Bert that if he did not leave me alone, he would be the one to get hurt. Aubrey lifted up his shirt and showed Bert his gun and warned him not to come near me again, telling Bert he had no problem defending himself or me.

Aubrey and I danced all night. We laughed, talked, and enjoyed our soda pops until it was time to leave. We made our way to the exit, talking about the upcoming grand opening of the barracks and going over the arrangements and activities. We were so engrossed in our own world, we did not see when Bert came out of the shadows until he tapped me on my shoulder and demanded I walk home with him. Aubrey stepped in front of me while covering me from Bert, and I told Bert to leave me alone or else. Aubrey's secret service men moved in and surrounded us, and Bert walked away. We all walked the short distance to drop me off, and my cousin took me into the house and saw me enter the bedroom. My family was awake. I got ready for bed and stayed in the room. I had difficulty sleeping because of the excitement with Aubrey and the upcoming grand opening.

Sleep eventually came, and so did morning. I prepared, got dressed, and gathered the things I planned to take on my trip to the barracks. Bert appeared out of thin air, saying, "You will not go to the grand opening… or else."

Worksite Visit

Bert knew of my plan to visit Aubrey's barracks, and he yelled at me and told me he heard about my trip to meet Aubrey on his job. He said he would hurt me and ridicule me in my community if I went and that Aubrey would be surprised. At that moment, my cousin approached, and I ran toward her with all my might. Bert backed off when he saw her, but he threatened me. "You'll be sorry later."

The trip was half an hour long, and the sight was beautiful. The trip was nature in its glory. The countryside was gorgeous. The air was crisp, fresh, and clean. The temperature was perfect as I traveled on the pickup truck. The sun was rising; the vapor lifting from the streams was rejuvenating. We traveled to Papaya through miles of untapped land with no houses, businesses, or civilization. This was one of the happiest days of my life seeing my friend Aubrey adapted well to living here.

When Aubrey saw the truck approach, he walked toward it. When he saw me, his smile expanded into laughter, and I could see his facial muscles relaxing. He lifted me out of the back of the truck with a quick kiss on my forehead. He put me to stand, and we stood there embracing each other, and at that moment, nothing else mattered. My cousin whispered my name, and Aubrey and I untangled ourselves and walked hand in hand toward the building where the grand opening was taking place.

Being Accepted by Strangers

Aubrey's cadets were standing at ease but at attention when they saw him approach. Aubrey introduced me to his cadets, his superiors, and the rest of the team. His superiors remarked that I stole Aubrey's heart. They teased, what magic had I worked on him? Aubrey's colleagues gave great reports about his character, and they said it had to take a lady with my charisma, charm, wisdom, and beauty for Aubrey to be so in love with any one woman. They went on to say they had never seen Aubrey so captivated, but they could see why Aubrey talked and felt the way he does about me.

It was time to eat. They had a large buffet to choose from. All different kinds of food and drinks were prepared. Barbecue chicken, vegetables, fried chicken, Chinese noodles, rice, fried plantains, cook-up rice, salads, spare ribs, fruit drinks, and all kinds of smoked meats. Aubrey asked me what I wanted to eat and to drink, and he fixed me a big dish and served me. After we ate, he took me on a grand tour of parts of the compound inside and outside. We walked the grounds, and he showed me the stream where they bathe and the other places where they get their water to drink and to cook. Aubrey and I were so excited, and we both felt such peace and contentment.

We spent the day together exploring part of the countryside and watching the birds and the wild animals, enjoying nature. The fruit trees were blooming, and fruits were everywhere. We played in the lakes and in the streams. We looked at and picked up small rocks and threw them into the water. We munched on snacks and spent time with his cadets throughout the day. Aubrey asked if I wanted to see his quarters and where he sleeps, and I said yes. Hand in hand, we walked back into the building, and Aubrey led me to his room. Everything was neat and perfect like the first time he opened his suitcase on the ship. The bed was made up with a white sheet with a dark-colored blanket folded at the foot of the bed. Aubrey's clothing and his toiletries were arranged on his dresser. His many bottles of colognes stood in order of size. I never saw a room so organized with nice colors and wall decorations. His room smelled so nice, and it felt peaceful and inviting.

Aubrey and I were still holding hands. He was such a perfect gentleman. He never took me for granted or took advantage of me. He never assumed because we spent lots of time together when his schedule allowed that he owned me or that I was his girlfriend. I never had another man treat me the way I was treated by Aubrey. Aubrey and I hugged, and it was the first time since we met that he asked me for a kiss.

Our First Kiss

We saw parakeets fly from branch to branch, and we felt the rays of the sun shining through the window on our faces. At that moment,

Aubrey asked me for a kiss. Our first kiss was magical. It took our breaths away. We kissed facing the open window overlooking the forest with the lake not far away. We could smell the aroma of the sweet, fresh water. We heard the parrots speaking and repeating conversations they heard. We were so captivated in the moment; we had no worry, no care, and no concerns. Kissing and being in the comfort of each other's arms and feeling secure and safe in each other was all we had.

I don't know how long we kissed or how long we were at the window. We were startled by a sudden noise on the outside. Aubrey and I released our grasp, and our kiss ended as we looked outside into Bert's angry eyes staring at us.

Our Moment Interrupted

Panic and fear took over me. I trembled. I did not know what to expect, but I could feel Bert was intending to do something bad. When Bert realized we saw him, he disappeared right before our eyes.

Aubrey hugged me and soothed my fear. Aubrey promised his secret service would escort me in the truck and that they would stay in the neighborhood as a precaution. Aubrey told me he would put in for leave time and come to visit in three days.

We spent the rest of the day exploring other parts of the outside of the compound. We decided to value our time together, and we continued to enjoy each moment. Aubrey told me I was the best thing that happened to him, and I also told him I felt so free to think and laugh and that he made it so easy for me to love him. We spent the rest of the day enjoying each other and sharing wisdom and insights.

And then it was time to leave. Our sadness was seen and felt by everyone. We did our best not to cry as we hugged, whispered, and embraced each other for as long as we possibly could. Aubrey and I walked hand in hand to the truck that was waiting to transport me back to my village. The ride back was painful for many reasons. We weren't going to see each other for three days if Aubrey's time off was approved. The pain of missing him was strong.

The fear of Bert pained me as well. Aubrey's secret service men and my cousin tried to cheer me up during the drive home, and I tried to respond in kind by looking at the beautiful countryside and the animals on my way back home.

When we reached my destination, my cousin and the secret service men came out of the truck. They checked the area, and when all was clear, they assisted me in getting out of the truck.

Hearing God's Voice

I felt nervous as I started the short walk to my family's house. Suddenly, the Holy Spirit whispered to me to run. I looked back and saw Bert hiding and began to run as fast and as hard as I could. Bert also began to run after me, but he couldn't catch me. I am a long distance track runner, and I ran for my school during the Olympics. I continued to run fast and hard, and I ran up the stairs and into the house, but Bert caught me right before I made it into the bedroom.

Bert grabbed me, began to punch me, and hit me all over my body with his fist as I fought as hard as I could. I threw shoes and anything I could at him, but Bert continued to assault me, and I became weak and collapsed on the floor. Bert kicked me with his boots, and blood oozed from my wounds and covered the floor. I fainted, and when I woke up on the floor later, I no longer felt Bert pouncing on and kicking me. I became aware that everything was still and quiet.

I struggled to sit, to stand, and gathered all my strength to clean up the floor from the blood. I went to bed and stayed in the bedroom until the next day. I reported the incident to my family and asked for Bert to be removed, but my family declined my request.

My Faithful Friend

Prior to Aubrey's visit, his secret service men came to check up on me, and I showed them the bruises. They were angry and wanted to take action, but I asked them to let Aubrey know what happened and that I was healing. I did mention to them that I was scared of Bert, and I left the house each day so as never to be alone in his presence. Aubrey's letter stated the day, time, and location to meet him on his upcoming visit, which I looked forward to.

True to his word, Aubrey got his time off and visited me. We met as planned, and I was so excited to see him.

When I went to hug him, Aubrey saw the bruises on my arms, and I cried out in pain. Aubrey was so upset, tears began to flow when he saw my bruises. Aubrey and I spent the day together. We had a beautiful picnic. The food was so delicious, and the weather was right as we lay on the beach and enjoyed the sunshine. Being with Aubrey gave me peace and contentment and made me feel safe. Aubrey and I decided our relationship was right for us, and we decided to get married when I graduated high school. We promised to be faithful to each other, and we would honor our virginity and not become involved until our wedding night.

We talked and laughed and ran on the beach, splashing water on each other until we were tired. Aubrey had a few days off, and we spent every second with each other. Aubrey himself took me to my family's home. We sat on the stairs outside and talked for many hours. Bert came and saw Aubrey, and Aubrey threatened him that the physical abuse he had done to me would be returned to him tenfold. I held Aubrey's hand and made him promise not to fight Bert. It took a lot out of Aubrey to agree to my request and for him to stay quiet about it. Bert stared at us, went into the house, and left us alone.

On Saturday, Aubrey came to my house, and we walked to the club. We danced and enjoyed the music and each other's company all night long. We loved being with each other.

As we are walking home, Bert snuck up on us again. "I've known her for a long time, and she never allowed me to hold her around her waist. Seeing your hand around her waist makes me angry."

Aubrey told him to leave us alone, and Bert again slinked away into the night.

Aubrey and I were inseparable. We went all over the country, enjoying the restaurants, the fruits, the waterfalls, and picnics at many of the different beaches. We had an awesome time together.

When it was time for Aubrey to return to work, we both wept. We had a hard time leaving each other. We held each other as though we would never see each other again. We hugged and tried to comfort each other, but only tears came. Parting was so painful.

The Belly of the Whale

The reality of Bert came flooding back after Aubrey's departure. I did not want to see or hear Bert's voice. I couldn't stand the thought of him. I felt unsafe with him around. I wondered when he would give up and leave. He knew I was never going to be his friend again. I wondered why he was still hanging around. I did not trust him. I wondered what he was thinking.

Then Bert appeared from thin air and started threatening me, telling me that if he couldn't get me, Aubrey couldn't have me either. From then on, I made sure I was never alone in the house with him.

One day I overslept and woke up to an empty house. Bert snuck up on me, wrestled me to the floor, and forced himself on me. He ripped my clothes off and raped me. He told me I better not tell anyone, or else. Afterward, I was terrified to be anywhere near him and was angry at my family for allowing him to stay and hang around, though I had asked them to tell him to leave. This was a very painful time for me. I never ever thought I would be raped in my family's house. I never envisioned losing my virginity to a rapist.

Aubrey and I promised we would remain virgins until our wedding night. I cried for a long time. I felt so dirty and couldn't believe what had happened. I did not want to go out any longer. Being raped took the joy out of my soul. My self-worth and selfesteem plunged to zero. I worried, suppose I am pregnant from this rape…what should I do? I didn't know how to share this tragedy with Aubrey. What would he think? I wondered. Would Aubrey still want me? I know I am the apple of his eyes and he loves me so much, and he knows I love him beyond words, but would our new love be able to handle this? And again, what if I'm pregnant?

I didn't know what to do. I felt the spark in me dimming. Aubrey continued to write, and though I was excited to hear from him, I didn't want him to see me, and I didn't want to be in his presence. During this time, I also had to prepare to return home as the time of my visit was coming to an end.

Aubrey and I continued to correspond in writing, and we planned on meeting up at my home in the city as soon as he took his vacation. Bert approached me and reported he was returning to the city as well, and he wanted me to travel with him. I ignored him. He said he would tell my family we had sex. I did not pick my head up to acknowledge his presence. He continued to taunt me and laugh at me and told me he would ridicule me in my village among his friends if I did not continue being his friend when I returned home.

Hiding within Myself

I returned home to the city, but with a different mindset. I felt I no longer belonged there. I was quiet about my vacation in the country and quieter about how I spent my time there. I became silent and withdrawn. I was not interested in going places or doing things I once enjoyed. I rejected invitations and lied about being busy working on a project. I thought about Aubrey a lot—the days we spent together on picnics, beaches, at nightclubs or just enjoying each other's company. I missed him, and I longed to hear his voice, consoling me and encouraging me and telling me everything will work out for our good. I am not convinced being raped is included in everything working out for my good.

I kept debating about whether I should tell Aubrey or not and what he would think about me if I did. Would he think I deserved being rape? Would he think I led Bert on to rape me?

So many times when a woman is abused, society feels the woman caused the abuse for one or more reasons. Many people would make comments such as the woman could leave, or she shouldn't have stayed in the relationship, insinuating that the trouble was her fault as well as his. Unless someone personally experiences the humiliation that comes from abuse, people can never know what this is like. Victims are embarrassed by the stigma from naysayers and family and friends when we're rejected. Society must know how we suffer from the effects of abuse.

I lost my virginity. All I could think of was the rape, and it made me so sad and angry. All the plans Aubrey and I made seemed no longer possible. I don't know if the love Aubrey and I shared would be able to handle the rape. I didn't feel it was fair not to tell Aubrey about the rape, and I didn't think it was fair to tell him.

Aubrey's last letter mentioned he was taking a week's vacation and coming to see me. He had his mother and other family members in the city, and he wanted me to meet his mother. I wanted so to see Aubrey, but I didn't know how to tell him about the rape. I didn't want Aubrey to continue with our relationship, though we made a vow not to keep secrets from each other.

Up until now, Aubrey and I communicated well with each other. If he still wanted for us to continue with our relationship and to marry, I didn't feel I would even let him marry me. I wanted Aubrey to hold me and to comfort me, but I couldn't bring myself to see him ever again. I felt Aubrey would become dirty if he hugged me. I wanted to present my body pure to my husband, to Aubrey. I couldn't accept the fact I was raped. I felt dirty about myself, and I began to take on a grim look on life and my future.

I felt like damaged goods, and I felt that I couldn't do anything about it. I longed to be in Aubrey's arms. I longed for us to be the way we were, but I didn't feel free any longer. Aubrey continued to write me, and I continued to respond to each of his letters. This made me sadder, and I became angrier with Bert.

Eventually, I wrote Aubrey to tell him that because of reasons I couldn't share with him, I was ending our relationship. I believed this would be best for both of us. I told Aubrey I would always love him in my heart and that I loved him beyond words. I asked Aubrey not to look for me or to write anymore.

My Last Letter to Darling Aubrey

This is my last letter to my love. I'm writing it in tears. The tears are flowing faster than my fingers can write the words on paper. This letter will confirm I love you far too much to allow you to endure the pain I feel when an incident shattered our plan. Aubrey, you are by far the best man I trust to share my thoughts and my dreams with. Being with you brought out the best in me and the hidden potentials in me. You exceeded my expectations and made me see things eyes cannot see and ears cannot hear.

Hon, you and I trusted and believed in each other in ways I believed no two people could ever share or know. You made me believe in myself, and this increased my self-worth, self-esteem, and self-confidence. Because of you, I know my sky is unlimited, and there are no boundaries I can't conquer. My potentials are limitless, and you made me realize it is not how many times I fall, but the fact that I dare to get up and try again. I will always be your queen, and you will always be my king.

I met you at a time of my life when I needed to feel safe and to feel worthy and to experience the touch of love from a male, and your touch is pure and true. Your touch provides me with pure intimacy without sexual intimacy. Most people would not believe the hours and days we spent with each other. Many people would believe a man and woman must be physically intimate if they spend so much time together. We proved them wrong. Many people also would not believe we kissed once and that this kiss sealed our relationship. We also proved intimacy can be enjoyed in a different way. I will always cherish the times we shared because they helped each of us to appreciate each other's spiritual gifts God blessed us with.

My desire and dream, my love, is to present my body holy and flawless to you on our wedding. Bert stole my desire from me. I will always love you. Though I don't know what God's plan is for us, I do believe our paths will cross again, and at this time, our goals and dreams will be realized, and nothing or no one could steal those from us. Continue on the path God assigned for you.

Aubrey did write to me several letters after he received my last letter, but I refused to respond. We never saw or heard from each other again. Meeting Aubrey is one of the best things to ever happen to me.

Crisis at Hand

I felt unsafe and tense with Bert hanging around, and I continued to withdraw myself from any activity or family gathering unless mandatory for me to attend. I didn't know how to tell my parents about the rape. Things I once enjoyed now brought me no pleasure. I dreaded being with the friends I made prior to escaping from Bert. I avoided Bert, and I didn't want anyone asking me about my relationship with him. I couldn't stand the sight of him, let alone hear his voice.

Bert, the rapist, was always at my house. He took every opportunity he got to parade in front of my family, who would refer to him as such a nice young man who is so manly and interested in me. I was nervous around Bert and would excuse myself whenever he was around or when I heard he was coming to visit my family. I stayed off the streets as much as possible and would go directly to and from school.

Bert became so manipulative that eventually, my family felt he was one of us, and they would share information with him and ask him for his opinions concerning my family's matters. Bert would volunteer to go to the store, run errands, and provide favors for my family.

Pregnant by a Rapist

Life for me became unbearable. I began to feel tired, hungry, and sleepy most of the time, and to complicate matters, I missed my menstrual cycle. This now became pure torture for me. My mind kept going back to the rape. How could I become pregnant from this rapist? It was bad enough he took my virginity, but to be pregnant by him! How could this be right? What a punishment! What was I supposed to do? What were my options being pregnant due to rape and having a baby out of wedlock?

And the rapist basically lived at my home. He was always there. I sometimes wondered if he still had a job or what arrangements he made with his company because he was always at my home. Every time I turned around, Bert was staring at me. Bert began to tease and jeer me about my boyfriend Aubrey. He wanted to know where Aubrey was. Bert reminded me of his promise to care for me, and he promised he was going to fix Aubrey real good. I was too afraid to know what that meant. Though I asked Aubrey not to contact me ever again, I cried long and hard and still wanted to know about Aubrey's whereabouts and how he was doing.

My biggest problem at the time was that I believed I was pregnant, and I had to find a way to approach my family. I didn't know how to do that or what the solution could be. Life can be so complicated and messy.

As I was looking for courage to find a way to tell my parents, my father came home and announced that his job had transferred him oversees, and only me, my mother, and the last child needed to be ready to leave within the month.

Transitioning into the Unknown

This had to be the best news I had heard since I returned from the country. Packing and preparing to leave my country took my mind from my terrible situation and gave me hope. I began to smile and laugh again and to share with my friends that I was leaving the city and did not know when I would return. I became encouraged because I knew Bert couldn't come where we were going, and I knew with time my family would forget about him. This pleased me a lot—the thought of not seeing him parading around my family anymore.

You should have seen Bert's face when he found out we were leaving the country, and he would have no access to me anymore. Bert tried to talk to me, but I pretended he was invisible. He tried his best to make himself useful by engaging my family in his schemes, but no one paid him any attention because my father kept us focused on our departure.

It was a pleasure for me to say goodbye to my teachers when I went to request my school records be sent to my new school.

I had to get a medical examination done. I was scared for the doctor to find out I might be pregnant. Luckily, I had had a physical before I went to the country on vacation. Therefore, all I needed was my doctor to complete my medical forms for immigration without having to take any blood work.

The night before we left Guyana, my family and friends came together and held a party. Many people attended, including Bert. It was fun to see them having a good time without bickering. I stayed far away from Bert and avoided him like the plague. He looked terrible, but I didn't say anything to him, good or bad. I wanted us to get on the plane to our new destination. During parts of the family get-together, I was nervous and hoped no one would ask me any questions. At the time, I had missed two months of my menstrual cycle. I was tired and always hungry and suffering from morning sickness. I kept my belly strapped down with a girdle and wore lots of skirts and loose blouses. No one in my family suspected anything, and I stayed away from the highlights of family and kept myself busy, always doing something to prevent me from sleeping or eating in the presence of others.

The day of our departure to travel to Venezuela came. Venezuela is located in South America. We got up early to travel to the airport and boarded an airplane that took us to Venezuela. I was not sure about the length of time my father's job would keep him working there.

This place was different from Guyana, and the people spoke a language I did not understand. Both of my parents spoke Spanish, and I spoke a little but understood Spanish more than I could speak it.

Things were different in this new country. It was becoming more apparent that I was pregnant because the morning sickness would wake me up, and I had to get out of bed. I suffered from being nauseous much more, and I became afraid to eat, in fear I would want to throw up and be unable to hide it from my parents.

One day my mother asked me if I was fine. She mentioned my color was different, whitish, and she did not remember the last time I reported having my menstrual cycle. This took me by surprise, and nausea overtook me. Before I could control my body, I began to throw up. I don't know if it was fear or relief, but the truth that I was pregnant was in the open, and my mother witnessed it.

The look on my mother's face was of horror. She was shocked and speechless. We had the conversation I feared the most. I was forced to let my parents know Bert raped me on my vacation in the country. I related the tragedy of how Bert came from behind and wrestled me to the floor by knocking me down and using his strong, muscular body and his legs to pin me down as he forced himself on me while ripping my clothing off and covering my mouth with a towel. I wept so hard and so long. My parents found a boarding home for pregnant teens and sent me away.

I remained there throughout the rest of my pregnancy and up until my daughter was born. My mother witnessed Martha's birth. My baby and I stayed there for three months, and then my parents came and brought us home. My parents told me they would take on all the responsibilities of Martha, and my mother had the boarding home prepare my baby's birth certificate and listed her name as the mother of my baby. My mother never allowed me to bond with Martha, and I was never allowed to tell anyone she was my baby. While living in the boarding home, I finished my high school requirements and got my diploma.

We stayed in Venezuela for over a decade. I went to the local college and graduated with a sociology degree and learned Spanish so well, I was speaking it as fluently as the natives. Many people thought I was from Venezuela because I learned the culture and adjusted well to the customs. My color and mannerisms are similar to the people of the land, and they accepted me.

During this time, I never returned to my native land Guyana, and neither did my parents. I never dated and always found an excuse when the Guyanese men living there asked me out. Martha was never told I'm her mother, and my family in Guyana thought Martha was my sister. I watched over Martha, but my parents never allowed us to get close, nor did they allow me to take her on any trips or to fuss over her. Martha grew up to be a beautiful young girl.

When my family from Guyana would visit, they updated my parents with all the gossip and news. They mentioned that Bert was still single and that he frequently asked about me. Bert never found out where I moved.

In my late twenties, my family became concerned that I was not dating. My heart longed for Aubrey, and I wondered what he was doing. But I did not know how to start looking for him, and besides, I didn't know if he would want to speak with me again. Therefore, I kept Aubrey in my heart and mind and tried to move on with my life while never stopping loving him.

One day my dad came home and announced the project he was working on was ending in a month, and his company was sending us back to Guyana. I was not sure if I should laugh or cry. I did not know how to react to this move. Though I was away from my native land for so many years, I did not make any significant friends in Venezuela who would want me to remain there. My father's company had a big house in the city furnished for us with all the amenities in the community. But again, we packed and were ready to return home. Our possessions were shipped out, and we boarded the plane and went back to Guyana after being away for over twelve years.

Coming Full Circle

I had been so relieved to leave Guyana over twelve years ago. Running from Bert and the abuse he inflicted upon my mind, spirit, and my body. Being raped by him because I refused to conform to his controlling demands and choosing Aubrey over him. No one but God and I knew the suffering and abuse I endured from Bert. I felt not only stripped of my womanhood but also scaled down to a zero, lost as I was in my confidence and self-esteem. I became so fearful and distrusting of men that I began to hide within myself.

Bert was a master manipulator. I saw him controlling the situations in my family's household as he played with my family's emotions. I wondered why I allowed myself to ever get involved with him. I ran from Bert into the safety, security, and comfort of Aubrey. I saw Aubrey as a man of valor. Aubrey is the king I fell in love with. Aubrey made it so easy for me to love him, and our desire was to be married. Aubrey is everything a woman would desire in a husband. He made me feel so safe and protected. We shared our dreams, goals, and visions, and our talks strengthened and restored my faith that a loving relationship with a man was possible. But all of that was so long ago.

Faith Comes by Hearing

God gave us instructions on how to live this life's journey. God's will and instructions for how we should navigate our lives can be found in

His Word, the Bible. In Romans 10:17, it says, "So then faith cometh by hearing, and hearing by the word of God." Aubrey and I communicated our goals and our visions of what we wanted to accomplish in our lives, individually and together. Because I kept hearing my goals and dreams I wanted to accomplish for my life, my faith was heightened, and this restored my self-esteem and my confidence. Aubrey and I spent so much time talking and encouraging each other as we planned our life together and planted the seeds for our future visions and dreams. However, we also promised to save ourselves as husband and wife. How sad that my vow to him could not be upheld.

I did not share this with Aubrey, my love. I was too afraid of any confrontation between Bert and Aubrey. Aubrey did not deserve to deal with Bert's abusive behaviors, and I would not be able to live with causing the interruption of Aubrey's life and future. He is a good man. I fell in love with Aubrey, and I knew he was in love with me. Aubrey's demonstrations and words deeply impacted my life—I know men can love and be faithful. I felt so blessed to be the woman Aubrey fell in love with. The hurt of being forced to leave Aubrey, the love of my life, was so painful, and this pain stayed with me for many years.

I always wondered what happened to Aubrey. We made plans, but I also know God's plans prevail. Aubrey and I made a vow to remain pure and not sleep with each other or anyone else. We made a covenant to save our virginity to be our first gift to each other on our wedding night. Our covenant became a part of my being. After being raped by Bert, I knew that because this vow could no longer be true, I couldn't marry Aubrey or let him know I was no longer a virgin.

I know Aubrey still would want us to be married, but I couldn't let that happen. I took away Aubrey's right to choose. I went through suffering and humiliation. I hid within myself when I realized I was pregnant with the rapist's child. I felt embarrassed and humiliated.

My parents lost trust in me and thought I was having sex with Bert and got pregnant. It is one thing to be abused and raped and then get pregnant. But it is heart-wrenching when your parents don't believe you, and you don't have anywhere else to turn. Because if your own parents don't believe you, who would?

The worst thing that came out of this pregnancy was that I was not allowed to bond with my daughter, Martha. To this day she does not know I am her mother. Only my parents and I know they are not her biological parents. Only I know the truth. How painful it is to watch your child grow up, and you're not allowed to do anything or to say anything to your child as her mother.

Returning to My Country

Traveling back to Guyana on the plane was so different this time. I had had many years to think and to process and to develop to get to know the most important person—me. I never thought of returning to Guyana or what it would feel like to face the demon Bert. I was going to have to face him again.

Emotional Responses to Abuse

The thought of having to see Bert caused me to be emotional. I began to feel sweaty, and perspiration dripped down my face and from my head down into my back. My breathing quickened. I began to take short breaths while gasping for air. I hyperventilated and had to calm myself. My face dripped with sweat, and as fast as I could wipe my face, the sweat continued to accumulate. My heart pounded so hard, I could see it moving my blouse. I could feel my skin become clammy, and I felt light-headed and dizzy.

I must have looked a hot mess because my mother turned to me and asked if I was feeling okay. I lied and said yes. This feeling stayed with me throughout the flight back to Guyana, and it was as though the flight back was longer than when we left Guyana. I nodded off because the next thing I heard was an announcement by the pilot that we needed to prepare for landing.

Flashbacks of Departure

I had flashbacks of who was at the airport to wish us well when we left Guyana. Many of my family and friends' faces appeared before me. Bert was also at the airport when we left Guyana. Time is bittersweet. I wanted to leave Guyana to start a new life. I grieved for Aubrey and the life we planned. Leaving Guyana and living in a foreign country made me bury my dreams and goals and the promises Aubrey and I made to each other. Over the years, I never thought about my family, and I missed them and our gatherings, our celebrations, our holidays, foods, and culture. I did not miss Bert, and I prayed he would not be waiting at the airport to welcome us back. God, help me!

Is This a New Start?

Our plane landed. After clearing immigration and customs, my family and I walked toward the exit, and a crowd of people gathered to meet us. My aunts, uncles, cousins, nieces, nephews, extended family, and friends were all there waiting to greet us. The crowd was so big, I did not recognize some of the people because my family now had a younger generation I had never met.

As my daughter Martha approached the crowd, a silence fell among the people gathered, and whispering began. My parents ignored this and kept walking toward them. My mother made an announcement, introducing her daughter Martha. Martha was big for her age, with long silky hair all the way down to her waist, and she was beautiful. Martha had a smile that would capture any person's heart. She was friendly, warm, and welcoming. She sure was a people person.

Her cousins approached her and introduced themselves. They grabbed her hand and carried her off to ride in their truck. I felt myself relaxing as I listened to the chatter from my family and friends. I was so happy Bert was not part of the welcome party. I wondered deep in my heart, have I forgiven him? Would I greet him if he were there?

The sunlight was so sharp and so hot, it cast a shadow over the gathering. My dad spoke with my family, and they informed him about the reservation at one of the famous restaurants built after we left.

Reconnecting with the Rapist

I don't know what I was thinking about, but I saw a shadow approaching. I recognized the face immediately—Bert.

As he came toward my direction, my peace and happiness turned to panic and anxiety. I became frustrated and wondered if Bert would ask questions when he saw Martha. Would he know she was his daughter?

My stress increased, and shame and embarrassment flooded my being. I became numb, and disbelief took over, and I was no longer sure returning to Guyana was the right thing to do. Bert stood in front of me, and I didn't know how to respond. He greeted me, saying it was so good for me to be back home. He asked, "How are you, Norah?"

I felt angry, and my mind drifted back to the day he raped me. I felt embarrassed and ashamed, responding after all those years to the trauma Bert inflicted as if it were yesterday. I had to remind myself that I did not deserve being raped, and none of it was my fault. Bert made a decision to hurt me, and he should be the one experiencing the embarrassment, shame, and guilt. Therefore, I picked my head up high as I continued to look him in his eyes and responded, "I'm amazing."

Suddenly, I heard my mother calling my name, and I walked in her direction to travel to the restaurant with them. I was quiet all the way to the restaurant and during most of the remainder of the day. Some of my family probed me about my time away and wanted to know what I had done and why I was not married yet. My family went on to inform me that many of the girls my age were married with children. My family was interested to know if I had any plans now that I had returned. I told them I needed time to become acclimated to the new culture in Guyana, and I had lots of things to think about now that I was back home.

My dad switched the subject, and my family filled us in about the different changes in our country and in the family. My family switched to Bert, lamenting that they didn't know why he was beginning to feel unhappy with this conversation, and I realized that my family's gossip was why I didn't miss them. Of course I made no comment to them in hopes they would stop talking or find something else to talk about.

The food was so delicious, and the ambiance at the restaurant was exquisite. The customer service was also awesome at this restaurant—unlike any I had ever experienced. I could see many things had changed since I left Guyana, and I felt I could be happy here despite how I felt about my family's gossip and the unpleasant feelings with Bert around. I was glad to be back home and needed to compare where I was when I left Guyana to where I was now in my spiritual, mental, and emotional life, and I wanted to adjust well to this environment.

Season of Transformation

In assessing my strengths and weaknesses and where I was at this time, I had to remember I survived the rape. Being raped is a painful and horrific ordeal. I had time in Venezuela to put my life back together, with the loss of the love and appreciation of Aubrey. What I realized from the rape was that it took a lot of strength to live through its aftermath. However, this event also strengthened a part of me that was negative—I was forced to lie about the daughter I conceived due to the rape, and I was forced to conceal her identity and to sign her birth over to my parents.

I knew the day was fast approaching when I would fight my parents to get my daughter back. Not one day went by when I was not haunted with the truth about my daughter's identity. My parents were deceptive during my times of vulnerability, and they took advantage of my situation. Nevertheless, Bert my abuser cannot take away the truth that not only did I survive the vicious attack of the sexual violence, I also displayed tremendous courage as I lived through the healing.

I realized I was not afraid of being in the same space with Bert, though of course, I resented him. My daily plan was to keep moving toward the goals I had set for my daughter and myself. I had never been involved with anyone before or after the rape. I survived the rape, shame, embarrassment, and pregnancy, increasing my strength, and yet this simultaneously did not cause a negative impact on me.

Soul-Searching

After coming to the realization that being violated by Bert was not my fault, I made up my mind to confront him. I had to plan how, where, and when I would do this. The more I thought about it, the more I felt the need to do it. I felt that by confronting, I could release built-up emotions and disappointment I had held on to. I felt I had to let go of the years of frustrations, but also hold Bert accountable for the abuse, vicious rape, and the consequences of that attack— our daughter—even though I couldn't tell Bert about her, not now, maybe not ever.

Confronting My Rapist

I don't know why I had such an urge to confront Bert, but I did. The thought of it was painful, and I experienced several nervous episodes with flashbacks of the abuse and my excruciating journey of telling my parents about the rape, the birth of my daughter Martha, and being deceived by my parents and losing my daughter to my parents.

One day I confronted Bert and told him that what he had done to me was wrong and that no person deserved it. I told him I did not give him permission to abuse me and to control who I chose to spend my time with. I let Bert know I hated his manipulative behaviors, such as befriending my family to get at me. Bert had problems hearing me talk about the rape and the emotional and physical abuse. Several times he attempted to distract me and to switch the conversation. Bert was more interested in whether I had reported the rape and begged me not to share this information with anyone.

He proceeded to tell me that I was confused—he didn't rape me. He said I was his girlfriend and that he just took what was his, and I made it difficult by fighting him.

As I listened to Bert, I realized his perception of the savage attack was twisted to favor what he thought our relationship was. So here I was holding Bert accountable, while he had altered the reality of raping me to avoid any guilt. His response hurt me further. Bert twisted the reality of the abuse, excusing it away, but I stood firm by telling him he did rape me and abuse me. I let him know I was not interested in him admitting his vicious assaults. I just wanted him to know how he treated me was wrong. He only tried to protect himself by denying the facts, but I knew the truth.

Confronting him empowered me. I told Bert that as I looked back over my life, his abusive tactics made me a stronger woman. I was now older, stronger, confident, and not afraid of him anymore.

Returning to My Abuser

ert took my confrontation as an invitation to speak with me every chance he got. He was interested in knowing about my plans and what my goals were now that I was home again. He tried to ask me personal things about the years I lived in Venezuela, but I never allowed the conversation to go there. I had casual conversations with him and kept those conversations basic. I avoided him, and if and when he visited my family, I chose those times to leave my home. The times when we did talk, he would frown. He told me he wanted us to talk, that he had had a lot of time to think about his life and what went on between us.

I said, "I need time to become accustomed to my native land because so many things have changed over the years. I don't have time for you."

I let Bert know I was going through a process because I needed to find myself and to make decisions about my future and where I planned to live and for how long. I reassured Bert that if and when I chose to speak with him about other things, I would let him know. But my needs were important to me—not his. I began to feel that because I was getting older, I should not fully close the door on Bert.

Time had passed, and I was not dating anyone because I was uncomfortable, and too many questions might be asked about my previous life in Venezuela. The reality hit me that I might be an old maid if I didn't do something—and fast. Many of the young ladies my age were married with children while I was not even dating. I was childless, or so they thought.

Holidays came and went, and I began to feel lonely and detached. My family and friends gossiped, calling me an old maid. I felt pressure from all sides. The truth was that I was not a virgin, and though I had built up resilience over the years, I couldn't avoid the nasty stares from my family and the people from my village. I couldn't come to a decision to date any other man, and because of the rape, I refused to marry any other person.

Bert became more persistent and continued to hang around my home and my family. The memory and the embarrassment of the rape continued, making me feel uneasy in his presence. Bert approached me about dating him, and in a time of weakness, I gave in and decided to rethink his offer. I made it clear we would not be physical before marriage, and I would not compromise.

We dated for six months, going places together and talking again. During this time, he finally apologized for the rape and admitted he was wrong to do those horrible things to me. I wanted to believe he felt bad for his abusive actions. He shared the abuses he had sustained as a child into his teenage years until he ran away from his home. I felt sorry for him and told myself that this was why he did those horrible things to me. I empathized with him and began to comfort him, seeing him as a victim like myself. Bert shared with me that he never felt love from his parents. His birthdays were never acknowledged, let alone celebrated. He received no gifts or good treatment from either of his parents. He confided that he felt like an outcast in his home and family and was the least among his household.

Married to My Rapist

Bert continued to hang around my family and me. He increased his visits to our home. My parents suggested I forgive him and give him a chance since I had no desire to expose my secret of losing my virginity due to rape and having a child. My parents' counsel made sense to me. I'm in my thirties and without a husband—not good. I began to feel so sorry for myself.

Bert and I continued to date, and when Bert asked me to marry him, I thought, *Well, I might as well marry him because he took my virginity anyway.* I hate what Bert did to me. I felt this was my best option, even though it was one I did not want.

As we began to prepare for the wedding, he was so happy while I felt trapped in this dark secret of rape and motherhood. I never shared with Bert that he is the father of my daughter. I did not feel he deserved to know, and I chose not to cause confusion in my daughter's life. Nevertheless, I knew one day I would fight my parents to get my daughter back. The night before the wedding, I cried for hours, and my parents knew it. They forced me to marry Bert anyway.

Taking Our Vows

Bert and I discussed how we wanted our wedding vows to be read, and I made slight changes for it to read, "I take thee, Bert, to be my wedded husband, from this day, for richer and richer, in health and health, in safety to love and to cherish, according to God's holy ordinance; and therefore I pledge thee my faith to you, Bert."

Bert and I were married in our church. Lots of my family and friends were there, and Bert's family and some of his friends attended. We went to Barbados for one week for our honeymoon. I had some challenges on our wedding night. I faked our lovemaking because the flashbacks of rape flooded my thoughts. I was not a virgin, but didn't feel so bad about this because my rapist Bert was now my husband.

Married Life

We moved into a nice neighborhood. My parents would visit, but my mother frequently showed up unannounced, upsetting Bert, and we argued about it. I reminded him that this was his behavior when he frequented my parents' home. Bert became angry with me and said they were fine with it. I refused to stay home. I got a job working in the school system teaching economics in high school. My job kept me busy, and that made me happy.

Bert and I coordinated the responsibilities of the home, and we did most of the cooking and cleaning together. Our jobs kept us busy, and I met new people I became friends with. This worked well for me because these people did not know me from before because they were not from my city or Bert's.

I felt peaceful developing my own desires and having my own opinions about things. Bert resented this and told me he wanted to be the only person to work. I disagreed with him and told him I had no problems caring for myself, and I didn't marry him to sit and watch the house. I made it clear I was interested in different things and would volunteer my time when needed, but would not neglect my duties as his wife. My school implemented many different kinds of fundraisers, and I started different clubs for teachers and connected well with them.

Bert continued to complain about my absence from home, so I encouraged him to do things with his friends and family. Bert and I spent lots of time together, but he wanted me to neglect some of my responsibilities with my colleagues, and I refused.

Feelings of Detachment

Bert complained a lot, and it appeared he was more displeased than ever. He insisted I quit my teaching job and spend more time caring for our home. I refused to do that and told him I did not marry to sit in a house all day or for the house to become my god. Bert complained that we were not pregnant. I reminded him children are blessings from God, and I am not God. I also said that maybe if he didn't rape me, I would be pregnant by now.

I am not the least interested in his desire, and in a way, I am pleased that things are not working out as he thought they should. Bert avoided speaking with me. His communications with me became short and harsh. He isolated himself and avoided eating meals or watching television or playing games together. He stopped attending church, while I continued attending church and became involved in the women's ministry. We no longer discussed plans, and whenever we were together, he would become moody. I did not care one bit as this gave me more room to become further involved with my projects. I also began to spend more time with my parents so I could see my daughter and know how she was doing. She was growing into such a beautiful girl, attending school where I teach. I was able to review her academic progress and discuss it with her teachers. She was taking honors classes and doing well. In addition, I tutored her in many of her classes and provided her supplies. I asked her not to share this with my parents, her grandparents. Of course, I couldn't tell her that particular detail.

Relationship with Parents

My parents asked me about Bert because he stopped attending our family's functions. "The man you forced me to marry, you mean," I would say. This upset my parents, so they began to inquire about him from other family members. My parents now made frequent visits to our home, and many of these were unannounced. My parents got his parents involved, which made Bert so angry. I was not the least bit bothered. I felt Bert and my parents forced our marriage, and now things were not working as planned for either of them—fine.

My parents became involved with reconnecting Bert and I and spending time with our pastor counseling us. Bert had no choice but to follow the instructions of our parents and pastor. He continued to sulk, but I ignored his behavior and mentioned to him that he needed to be careful what he asked for. Many times when we get what we want, we are still miserable. I was happy that Bert was unhappy and couldn't get things his way. I continued being responsible for my duties as a wife and mother and did not allow Bert's behavior to dampen my outlook. I began to feel well and more comfortable with Bert. I even began to see some positive changes in him, or so I thought.

Bert became agreeable and more responsible, and he returned to church and became involved in the men's ministry.

Pregnant by My Rapist Husband

I was so busy and involved in the daily activities at work, in my community, and with my family that I did not realize how tired I was feeling. I felt drained and sleepy and couldn't figure out why. I was in excellent health, though my relationship with Bert was not working out well. I continued to be so involved and busy that people would ask me how I was able to get so many things done. I never stopped to assess what was going on. I only knew I had things to complete. I received the Teacher of the Year Award and many other awards at church and in the community from businesses. I began to feel more tired and nodded off during dinner. Bert noticed and suggested I see my doctor; maybe I needed some kind of supplement because my activities had increased. I tried to brush it off, but Bert insisted and scheduled an appointment and accompanied me. After my doctor examined me and took blood and urine samples, he announced, "You are three months pregnant."

Astonished and speechless, I did not know if I should laugh or cry. Bert jumped up and laughed uncontrollably as he hugged and kissed me.

He called our parents to share this exciting news. I had great difficulty accepting the pregnancy because I felt things were about to change between us. Bert wanted us to celebrate, but I preferred not to. We ended up ordering food and staying home. Bert wanted us to plan for our baby, and I declined. I wanted to get the things on my agenda finished because I began to feel overwhelmed. Unsure of who or what to avoid, I refused to allow myself to think of the pregnancy.

Season of Change

Bert became insistent and demanded we begin to set plans in place for our baby. I was worried that Bert was going to use our baby to force me to leave my job and family to get a bigger home and to change our location. Bert had wanted us to move for the longest time because he complained my parents were always coming over to our home, and he assumed they did not trust him to care for me, which upset him. Bert said he loved me and would never do anything to hurt me or to jeopardize my safety. Really! I guess he has forgotten.

I had a hard time believing him because he did rape me and made me pregnant once, unknown to him. I felt he had changed, but I knew he could become destructive and harmful, even when unprovoked. Therefore, in the back of my mind, I had a feeling he would do it again if he were pushed, but I did not know how or when this could happen.

I continued with work and ministry, but I began to slow down with my other community activities. Tiredness overwhelmed me. Morning sickness was frequent. Getting a larger living space became a top priority. Bert wanted us to relocate out of Guyana, but I refused. This made him adamant, and he continued to pressure me every moment about starting over in another country. We settled for a bigger place ten miles away. Next, he wanted me to quit my job and stay home. I refused to give up my freedom and instead urged for us to look into childcare for our baby.

I continued teaching up until my ninth month, which worked out well as this coincided with my summer vacation.

Our Angel Came Home

Our beautiful daughter, Angelica, made her grand entrance into the world. My labor pains were fierce and sharp, and they lasted about twenty-four hours nonstop. Bert took me to the hospital when the labor pains became severe and intense. I screamed and wept throughout the labor. I wanted an all-natural delivery, but I requested medication to relieve the severe discomfort of the pressure. Beautiful Angelica weighed eight pounds, measured twenty-one inches, peeked at the world with gray eyes, and shone with the most beautiful pink complexion. This became a moment of pure joy for our family. I believed when the nurse placed my angel on my tummy and I held her, at that moment, the reality of motherhood was sealed this time.

I held my baby for a long time and wept uncontrollably, and no one knew what happened. When the nurse came to take my baby, I began to scream, "No, you can't take her! She's mine!" I had flashbacks from when my first baby, Martha, was taken away from me and coveted by my parents as their own daughter. I lost all rights to bond or to form a relationship with my first daughter. My parents forged their signature on her birth certificate by paying off the medical staff in Venezuela, and my daughter still does not know I'm her mother. I did not tell Bert she is his daughter.

The medical team and Bert looked at me. They didn't know what to say or do. I continued to hold my baby, and with some negotiation from the medical team, I relaxed and believed their promise to bring her back to me. Bert stood next to me speechless, and for a moment, my doctor didn't know what to say or do because my crying was uncontrollable.

I never shared this reaction with anyone. Neither did I plan to do so. Our family and friends supported our baby and us, and they provided assistance to us around the clock. My mother moved into our home and provided lots of help with chores. Bert became unhappy with this, and I could see and feel his frustration with my family. He complained to me a few times, but I asked him if he was willing to quit his job to help out with the care that was needed at this time. Bert was quiet, but my family's presence still did not appeal to him.

Upon Angelica's birth, things got better between Bert and I, and I wanted us to be a real family. Our baby grew stronger and bigger and began to achieve her developmental milestones in record time. I felt my life had taken on a new meaning, and I loved being a mother. My baby became my joy, and I loved every moment spent with her. Bert assisted in the care of our daughter, and he spent lots of time with her. Bert and I took turns getting up during the night to attend to her needs. Our daughter became our joy, and Bert insisted my family didn't need to be around as often. I encouraged him to talk with them, and they listened and reduced the time they spent at our home.

Things felt even better between Bert and I. I began to tolerate him a little more, and I even started to like him and then even fell in love with him for the first time since he raped me.

Bert wanted me home and insisted I quit my teaching job to care full-time for our baby, but I refused. Instead, we went and interviewed day-care centers and staff, and we chose a day-care center we both felt comfortable with. I returned to work the first day of school and felt great being back with my colleagues. The first day, I received a promotion at work as a facilitator in the leadership program. I had new things to learn, and lots of training of new staff was included. I conducted many workshops and became a part of the new mentorship program, coaching first- to third-year teachers. I loved this so much because I was able to provide help to teachers in areas of their need, and this improved teachers' retention rates. My salary increased over twenty thousand dollars. Bert was not happy for me, but I did not allow this to be a bother. Our daughter adjusted well at day care, which was apparent to everyone who saw her. At our home, things seemed quiet. It made me uncomfortable. Bert was either in agreement or pretending to be.

I did not know where or how things were changing. *Here it comes,* I thought.

The Storm Is Here

One moment I am laughing and so happy, and the next moment hurricane Bert showed up. Bert announced to me that his job is relocating to French Guiana within six months, and we will be moving there. I gasped when I heard him. When I composed myself, I said, "You need to start looking for another job here because I'm not going with you."

He looked angry and screamed, "You are my wife and will do as I say!"

"Yes, I'm your wife, not your slave!"

We kept screaming back and forth about ten minutes and only stopped when we heard the screams coming from our daughter Angelica. Our fights had just begun.

Bert and I argued about everything, and we had great difficulties listening to each other. Nothing was accomplished between us. We lived like strangers under the same roof. Angelica's mood changed. She was cranky and cried when she was dropped off at the day-care center. The day care reported that she no longer played with the other children but stayed in a corner, watching the other kids play. The day-care staff also reported that she often cried and many times did not want to eat or drink.

My world was changing right before my eyes, and I couldn't do anything about it. Bert and I spoke to discuss finances or bills. At work, my friends shared that my attitude changed, and they inquired if everything was going well. I shared with my close friends that Bert wanted us to move to French Guiana in six months, and he refused to look for another job here. My friends were shocked and sad and stated they didn't know what to say or do. My family also noticed discord between Bert and I, and they inquired about our relationship. I shared the dilemma that Bert refused to look for another job in Guyana and insisted we moved to French Guiana. My parents came by several times to speak with Bert. Some of the times he avoided them, and other times he refused to listen or to reason with them. Bert told me he accepted the new job and that I need to quit my job and pack. I refused. "I am not going to quit or take our daughter out of the day care."

Bert's anger flared, and he shouted he would seek custody of our daughter if he had to because he planned on leaving with her.

I spat out, "You can if you want, but I contacted a lawyer who told me the court will not give you custody of our daughter. I will petition the court to prevent you from receiving custody to relocate my daughter to French Guiana."

Bert's whole demeanor changed, and his expression was one of shock. When he did speak, he told me he would leave, and I could travel at the end of the school year. I withheld from asking Bert what would happen if I chose not to go away with him ever. I decided not to ask him that because I wanted peace with my family. I felt I had invested a lot in this relationship.

The New Country

Things became peaceful again. Angelica returned to her happy self at the day-care center. Bert and I had lots of things to do within a short time, and I helped with Bert's packing and getting his paperwork in place. I made his medical appointments and made sure he had his travel documents current. He didn't know how long he would be there before he returned on visits, and I didn't want to cause a rift between us by bringing this up. Angelica suspected some change with her father, and she began to cling to him often. I could see Bert struggling with leaving, and I needed him as much as I did not feel I did. I felt we had come a long way in this relationship.

Our families, friends, and I got together and threw a huge farewell party for Bert. Many of his friends and coworkers were present.

The party became bittersweet. Some people were crying, and others were laughing, and Bert's coworkers attended in record numbers. We had a great time, and before we knew it, it was time to travel to the airport to see Bert off. Angelica refused to leave her father's lap and hugged him all the way to the airport, and when it became time to say our goodbyes, she cried and I cried. I never thought the day would come when I would cry to see this man leave, but I did, and Bert also cried. The occasion became sad, and my last words to him were, "You are too stubborn to find a job here, but you won't listen to me."

He boarded his plane, and away he went. Bert's housing and car were in place in French Guiana when he got there. We corresponded quite often. He began his new job and received a promotion and had lots to learn, including the new language and culture. Bert visited at the end of his second month, and we shared the weekend together. It appeared so much had changed since we last saw each other. Angelica displayed pure joy to see her daddy. She talked nonstop, telling him about her friends at day care and what happened at church in her Sunday school classes.

Time flew by fast, and soon Bert had to leave, and again our goodbyes were sad, except this time it was only the three of us. Bert anticipated we would all join him at the end of the school year. I was not comfortable about this and felt overwhelmed. I did not want to leave my job, my family, and my friends to start my life from scratch. I did not want to be a stay-at-home mother.

Bert sensed my apprehension and asked if I had given in notice to leave before I went on summer vacation. I shared with him that I hadn't because I did not, in my mind, want to relocate with him.

Bert was quiet for a moment. He said, "I will be traveling home in a few days, and we can talk later."

During this visit home, Bert and I argued and disagreed a lot because I refused to resign my position. I felt weird leaving everything I was accustomed to and enjoyed. I began to see flashbacks from when my family and I traveled to Venezuela many years ago.

I wanted to get away then from the embarrassment of Bert raping me and me getting pregnant. Leaving then wasn't a bad thing, but feelings of sadness over Aubrey engulfed me. Bert became angrier by the hour, and he threatened to take me to court to get custody of Angelica. This did not rest well with me. I became afraid of what might happen if the court ruled in his favor, and he did get joint custody. After much disagreement, I acquiesced to relocate to French Guiana. I told my family and friends that I would be joining Bert in French Guiana in the summer, and they reacted with shock. I prepared my resignation letter and gave it to my school. Bert took time off from work and returned to help with the arrangements and packing. My family was upset with him and avoided him and ignored him. Needless to say, our time to leave Guyana approached, and before we knew it, we were traveling to our new home.

To the Unknown

I wasn't sure what to expect in this new country. I did not want to be a stay-at-home mother. But I was unaware about the communities and what to expect or how things were going to come together for me. I adjusted to my new environment, though it appeared the shopping, stores, schools, and places of worship were far away. I struggled to interact and to connect with the natives. It was difficult for me to connect with the people; they didn't speak English, and I didn't speak French. We had a language and culture barrier.

Bert was gone all day, and I was feeling frustrated as the weeks went by. I grew angry with him, and we spent most of our time together disagreeing and arguing. I felt disconnected from everything and everyone, and Bert insisted I stay home. This made me unhappy, but options were limited since I didn't know the language and was unfamiliar with how things were done there.

Enrolling my daughter in school was a task. I did not like where we lived. Transportation was challenging because I was not driving, and the public transportation service was unreliable, poor, and expensive. Because of the language barriers, I did not feel comfortable taking the private transportation services. Most of the time I was stuck in the house until the weekends when Bert was available for us to go shopping. Many of Bert's coworkers from Guyana lived in the city, and Bert took up housing far into the country.

After being in French Guiana for a month, Bert started hanging out with the men from his job, and he would come home late and sometimes intoxicated. This frustrated me, and we continued to disagree with physical fights. Loneliness settled upon me, and I was beginning to feel the way someone in jail feels, a prisoner in my house and in the country. Bert wanted us to keep to ourselves, and I had no contact with his friends' wives, not even during the holidays. The phone services were expensive, and calling my family and friends back home was a challenge. Bert rationed the money for the house, and so now we argued over not having enough money. My savings account depleted so that I had to depend on Bert. He refused to move closer to the city where many teaching positions were available. He remained adamant about me not working and insisted that I homeschool Angelica. I began to feel ill, tired, and weary, and I connected this with stress from the move and his explosive outbursts, arguments, and abusive behaviors.

His Way or the Highway

He became temperamental and now graduated to abusing me by calling me mother f——, b——, stupid, and no-good wife who can't do anything right. Bert took to assaulting me by pushing, slapping, throwing things, or pushing me out of his way off our bed when I refused to become intimate with him. I threatened to report him to the police, and he laughed in my face, telling me they wouldn't believe me because the husband had a right to enforce discipline on his wife to keep her in line.

I decided to save up some of the house money and buy a calling card to call my parents, which I did during one of our grocery trips into the city.

I was speaking with my parents on the phone when Bert intercepted the call and dragged the wires from the wall. He grabbed what was closest to his hands and threw it at me when I opposed his ideas. Or if his dinner was not ready and he couldn't eat right away, he would become enraged. Or if he didn't like the food, he would throw the plate across the floor. Many times I had to duck to prevent injury to my body. I felt so tired, and to my surprise, I began to experience morning sickness. I became so angry at the possibility I might be pregnant. I was planning to leave him for good, and now another child would make this impossible with little to no money or resources. So many things crossed my mind, even thoughts of having an abortion. But how would this be possible, where would I go, or where would I get the money? Worse, what would Bert do to me if I had an opportunity to abort our baby, and he found out?

I was becoming more afraid of him and his escalating temper. I planned not to tell Bert about the possibility I may be pregnant. I started skimming on the bills' money and paid minimum payments. Bert would never know because he was too busy getting drunk with his friends and doing what he wanted when he wanted. I needed a doctor because I didn't understand the language and didn't know who to talk with, let alone who to trust.

Fears Came Through

Morning and night sickness became frequent, and the symptoms of pregnancy were evident. I kept hoping this was a bad dream, and my body was just reacting to stress with tiredness. My suspicions of pregnancy became stronger due to the feelings I experienced. I didn't want to keep my pregnancy a secret from Bert because if he found out, he would not trust me and would feel I was keeping secrets from him, which would create additional problems for me. I had to come up with a plan.

Bert wanted more children, and I didn't want any more children from him. I had been on birth control not to get pregnant, but when Bert found out, he went crazy. He cursed and screamed, and Angelica and I were so scared, I grabbed her and ran into a closet to get away from him. This pregnancy was unplanned, and I knew it would hinder me from executing my plans to escape him. I also knew I must tell him soon to avoid additional problems in our marriage. I mustered up my courage and told Bert during dinner, "We are pregnant."

He jumped out of his chair, ran toward me, and began to hug and kiss me. He made all kinds of promises and told me he wants us to improve our relationship. I was unsure what to believe, but of course, I prayed he would keep them this time. We made arrangements for a doctor's appointment, and he took time off from work to accompany me. He was so excited while I showed no emotions. I couldn't believe I was pregnant. This made me angry, sad, frustrated, and disgusted, but I had no choice because my unborn child didn't ask to be born.

The Grace to Endure

Coming back from the doctor with the confirmation of pregnancy, Bert's behavior became a little more tolerable.

On the way home, he stopped in the store and bought me ice cream and snacks that he knew I liked. His behavior was easier to tolerate. He didn't want me to lift anything, and he didn't want me to cook either. From work, he would be right home caring for Angelica and me. He cooked, cleaned, and made sure my needs were met. Bert set the bathwater and rubbed my back and body as he gave me tub baths, then dried and lotioned my body. I whispered to him, "You are spoiling me, and I could get used to this royal treatment."

We got along better. Bert said *please* and *thank you*, which wasn't usual for me to hear. Morning and night sickness were bad. Many times I couldn't eat food to prevent morning sickness. Bert claimed he was worried about me, and I overheard him saying to his friend he never saw me experiencing morning and night sickness because I am very independent. He told his friend he would hire his wife to come during the daytime to help care for Angelica and to help me around the house because he didn't want anything to happen to me.

Help Is on the Way

Bert spoke with his friend who left Guyana with him, and they agreed that his wife, Myra, would come to help me with childcare and housekeeping. Bert retained Myra, and she worked well, and her presence made me feel less lonely. She took care of Angelica and did all the chores in our home. I still spent time with Angelica teaching her because she was homeschooled. Myra told me that Bert volunteered to travel to this country and refused to accept a job his boss had arranged with another company. Myra wanted to know why I left my family when they were assisting with the care of my daughter. She spoke about how wonderful it must have been for me to teach in the local school district and to have earned the new promotion.

I was stunned by this, and before I could respond, in walked Bert through the back door, just in time for her to change the conversation. How much Bert had heard of our conversation, I didn't know, but it took effort for me to contain my anger at this new information.

Bert cooked, yet many times I couldn't eat. My diet had become so unpredictable due to throwing up. My appetite was poor, but my doctor was not worried. Bert and I knew this baby is a boy, and Bert was thrilled. This was the first time I ever saw my husband doing the things a husband should. I relaxed with him. During these times, I changed my mind about wanting to escape from him. I had the conversation with Bert about us moving to the city, sending our daughter to a school where she can interact with kids her age, and me returning to work. Bert agreed, which brought some peace to my spirit. I began finding out about jobs so I could position myself when the time came for me to transition back to work and to know my money is mine.

Emotional Impact

The due date of our son approached, and Bert became a nervous wreck since his best friend's wife had lost her baby at birth. The baby was a boy. Bert called home every chance he got. He was worried about the pregnancy. If my assistant answered the house phone, Bert demanded to know where I was. If she told him I was in the bathroom, he made her knock on the door to give me the phone. At nights, Bert would not sleep unless his hands and feet were entangled with mine. This was uncomfortable and made me nervous because I was unsure of his intent. He needed reassurance. Bert would wake me up at night, rubbing my tummy, and our baby would enjoy the touch of his father's hand. Bert spent time talking and singing to his son. I would wake up tired because Bert would only have peace if he were snuggled next to me. Bert was never tired, and I saw such a transformation with him during these times.

This pregnancy was different from my others. I was restless with terrible morning and night sickness and also had bad cravings. But Bert acted the role of the perfect husband. I don't know if it was because I was pregnant with our son, or because we were in this strange country away from families. One day I decided to ask Bert about his closeness with this baby.

Bert Has Spoken

My husband told me he never felt able to bond with Angelica because my mother was always at our home. Bert told me he never felt he could speak with me unless my mother approved the conversation. He said my mother was always involved in the affairs of our lives and my pregnancy. He felt he needed approval from my parents to be my husband, and this upset him. I responded, "Why do you think that is?"

He gave me a blank stare. I shared with him where things were between us. I told him about the savage way he raped me while assaulting me and tying my hands and knocking me down because I refused to conform to his demands of being in a relationship with him. I wanted Bert to hear how I felt when he attacked and humiliated and tortured me. My parents and community rejected me. I shared with Bert how I told my parents about these incidents because he shared with his friends how he raped me. His friends shared this with my peers I went to school with, and it got back to me. I told Bert I was happy for my dad's promotion to relocate to Venezuela. During that time, I was able to reflect on how Bert abused me and stripped me from my womanhood and took away my dignity. I reminded Bert that women do matter because I do matter. I let Bert know how I felt about him and that I had no desire to ever be with him, let alone marry him.

Bert looked dumbfounded with this information. He changed colors before my eyes. He began to sweat, and the more he wiped the sweat, the more it poured.

Why Marry Me?

When he did speak, he asked, "Why did you marry me?"

I replied, "Because you had damaged me and stripped my fiber and my oath to present my body pure to my husband. You damaged me when you raped me and took my virginity. You frighten me, but you don't intimidate me, even though you try. No one intimidates me. However, after this painful and sinful ordeal, I felt like damaged goods, and I refused to be with anyone else. Therefore, I returned my damaged body to you because you raped me."

Bert was shocked, and he began to cry. I couldn't lift a finger to comfort him or to wipe his tears. I wanted him to feel the anguish I felt all these years. He sat at the end of the bed and wept for a while, and

I also laid on the bed and wept, but for different reasons. When I did speak, I said, "When we first met, I liked you until you began to abuse me. I needed to escape from you to give me some time to decide whether I wanted to remain friends with you and to give you time to get yourself together."

Bert then asked me what I always knew he wanted to ask me— he asked about Aubrey.

What Happened to Aubrey?

"Did you get physical with Aubrey?"

I said, "Never. When you saw Aubrey and me kissing, that was the first and the last time we ever kissed, and it was the only moment of intimacy we shared. I am in love with Aubrey because he protects me, and he is kind and generous. Aubrey wants some of the same things I want, and he is a distinguished gentleman. I trust him with my life."

I reminded Bert that the only reason I connected with Aubrey was because I needed to escape his torment and because he refused to change his abusive behaviors. I asked Bert, "What happened to Aubrey and the letter he wrote to me when I returned to the city?"

Bert said, "You don't need to worry about Aubrey or the letters anymore."

I said, "You're right, I don't, but you should because until I know what happened to Aubrey, you will always wonder and worry. After the rape, I tried not to think about Aubrey anymore, and I felt the release and tension leave my spirit. I knew that if Aubrey and I were to ever meet, it would happen because God wanted it to."

Bert apologized and said, "I thought Aubrey and you were intimate. I became revengeful by raping and abusing you when I found out you and Aubrey were spending time together."

I replied, "You can't stop what God puts together and blesses."

Divine Interruption

When I felt sharp pains in my belly radiating down my lower back, the next moment, I was screaming, and I could feel the pains becoming more intense. Then I felt my water bag erupt. Bert looked frightened, and when he did speak, he said, "But our baby is not due until two months from now."

I screamed, "Wake up, Angelica!"

Bert ran to Angelica's room and woke her up, and he ran back into our bedroom, grabbed me up into his hands, and carried me to the car. Bert called my private doctor to say we were on our way. Outside was dark, and some of the streets had no lights. My Angelica held my hands and comforted me as her dad drove recklessly; she was trying to comfort me and tell me everything was going to be all right. I couldn't respond because the pain was severe and coming every three minutes apart. Angelica began to cry and asked if I was going to be okay. Bert answered, but his voice shook, and he was crying. Bert tried to comfort me, but he was sobbing and begging me not to cry and to stay calm because he didn't want anything to happen to me or to our baby.

The pain was so intense. I was rocking, moving, and weeping as Angelica tried to comfort both of us.

Bert pulled up at the hospital, and the staff set me on the stretcher and rushed me into the hospital delivery room. My doctor examined me as I was screaming. The pain agonized my tiny body of 120 pounds. My doctor sent a nurse to call my husband to inform him that our baby was in a breech position with the cord around his neck. Bert looked confused and wanted to know what would happen to us. The doctor told him to be calm and started to explain the procedure, but Bert screamed as he collapsed on the floor. My doctor ordered medical care for Bert, and although he was revived, he was not allowed to come back into the delivery room.

Struggling to Be Born

My doctor and his team continued to work on delivering my baby alive. The delivery took a long time. My son's position changed from breech to the birthing position, and the cord was removed from around his neck. The pain was severe, and I fainted. I don't recall what happened next, but when I woke up, I felt my belly to find my baby was no longer there. I was in a different room, and neither my husband nor my children were with me. I rang the bell for a nurse, and she appeared. She assured me everything was fine, and my husband and daughter were just outside the nursery watching our newborn baby. My heart leapt with faith.

Faith Comes by Hearing the Word of God

I removed the tubes attached to my body and limped my way to the nursery and joined my family. When Bert turned around and saw me, he walked toward me with arms outstretched. I embraced my husband and wept on his shoulder.

Angelica ran toward me. "Mommy! Mommy! Are you fine now?" Tears were rolling down her cheeks. She joined us in the embrace, and we all wept in the presence of each other. This was the first time I felt a true embrace from my husband, and I didn't want this moment to end. I felt safe and protected. I felt I could love my husband, and I wished we could always be this way as a family. At that moment, I wanted my marriage to work and to last and for my family to remain intact. I felt I could let Bert know about our oldest daughter. Although I didn't know how this would affect him, I planned to get my daughter from my parents.

Our Premature Baby

The medical team did not prepare me for what to expect when I first met my baby. He was so tiny, and I saw him with tubes all over his body, lying lifeless. I was speechless to the point of panic. I screamed in disbelief for all I could see were tubes. I wept so hard, the medical team approached us and guided us into an office to talk with us. I continued to weep while my husband comforted me.

Discussion about Prematurity

The doctor spoke to us and explained that our son, Bert Junior, was born premature at twenty-eight weeks. We were told that his survival rate was more than 95 percent. Once I heard this, I stopped crying and felt fear leave me, and I became hopeful. The doctor said our baby would need lots of medical care and attention and would remain in the hospital for a while because he had lots of premature organs. Bert Junior needed to grow taller and to gain weight. The doctor said our son might be at risk for developmental problems and behavioral problems later in life. The doctor also recommended that Bert and I speak with a counselor because the stress of having a baby with medical risks can cause psychological and marital distress. My husband told the doctor we needed a moment to discuss these things and would get back to him.

Our baby stayed in the hospital for many months, and he grew stronger and developed his organs to fight pneumonia, colds, and other illnesses. Our son's medical condition impacted Bert's and my relationship in negative ways, placing a strain on us.

Marriage Falling Apart

Bert and I became tired coordinating the hospital visits during the week. Because I did not have my own transportation to visit my baby during the day, I had to wait for Bert to get home from work to visit. Sometimes Bert would go visit without me, which angered me. Angelica became tired and withdrawn because I was unable to provide her homeschooling as planned or to spend quality time with her. I was tired most of the time and snapped with low tolerance for frustrations. I lacked sleep and was not eating well. I approached Bert about us speaking to a counselor and getting help to do chores around the house to free up some of my time. Though it was crystal clear that we needed help, according to Bert, we were doing fine.

Frustration was all over us because of the difficulties coping with the extra stress of our son's health and medical conditions. Bert Junior was still in the hospital after four months, and his discharge date was still unknown. We needed help because the household chores were behind, and sitting down to write out and pay bills on time and keeping our many appointments became impossible.

Bert wanted to visit Bert Junior during the workdays, while Angelica and I were to visit on the weekends only. This arrangement was unacceptable to me. I grieved not being able to hold my son, let alone breastfeed him and to bathe and dress him and to talk to him and to let his sister bond with him. I became so sad and disheartened with my son's long hospital stay and with Bert continuing to either yell, scream, curse, or increase his drinking. Loneliness and feelings of being so overwhelmed festered and grew.

Lonely in Marriage

It is said that when two people are married, a man shall leave his mother and cling to his wife, and they become one. In my mind, I take this to mean no more loneliness. This is God's Word, written in the Bible, yet many people don't feel the need to honor it. Married to Bert, I felt more alone and isolated than ever before, living in this strange country away from the people I know and the customs of my culture. The connection between Bert and I was no longer there because we were not close. Our marriage began on unstable ground. The circumstances that brought us together were not love but embarrassment.

Many times we want to place a square in a round hole, which does not work. Or sometimes we marry for the wrong reasons and think this marriage will fix whatever is wrong, but it does not work that way. Jesus Christ is the solid rock we stand on because all other ground is sinking sand, and I can see and feel the sinking all around.

I reached a place in our marriage where I didn't know if I wanted to invest much into it. I wanted my baby to be made whole and to be discharged from the hospital, and I needed to deal with the issues in my tissues that were still there—the rape and secret birth of my first child. Our daughter didn't know we were her parents, and this was wrong. I didn't want to upset her whole life, but again, it was not my fault for not telling her. Martha needed to know she was an older sister to two young siblings. My mother told me Martha had become quiet, distant, and spent so much time in her room with the lights off.

Many marriages go through ups and downs like the seasons; some hot, some cold. My marriage experienced hardships, rough times, and domestic abuse. I became accustomed to his screams, curses, and accusations for causing his son to be in the hospital because I neglected myself. Our marriage was crumbling fast, and I felt my efforts were useless. Bert and I communicated only when necessary; otherwise, we argued about almost everything. I was tired and fatigued, but loneliness and worry prevailed. Bert hung out more often after work with his friends and often came home drunk. Bert said that after visiting our son, he would meet his friends and go out drinking. Bert told his friends we still love each other, but that I was occupied by priorities that take up most of my time. I made friends with some of the women in my community, and they were so understanding of my plight that they began to take turns taking me to visit with my baby without Bert knowing.

Bert Junior made improvements, and some of the tubes attached to his tiny body were removed. I was unable to breastfeed or to hold him. I spent my time talking to my son, touching his body, and knowing that he recognized my voice. This was so painful to watch my son, so tiny, but unable to hold him or care for him. During my visits, I made sure that Angelica spent time with her brother, and then I would spend quality time with Angelica in the town doing something she liked.

Sad and Lonely

The disconnection between Bert and I became stronger, and we seldom did much together. I didn't know where to turn or whom to talk with. I believed he blamed me for our son's medical problems. I needed to talk with anyone who would listen; therefore, I asked for help from the wives in my community. I wanted to share the discontent I had been experiencing with Bert's frustration with Bert Junior's hospitalization.

Some of the women related to my story and shared how they experienced many of the same things and didn't know what to do. Some felt the only reason I was lonely was because I was searching for love. I believe love is profound, and it should be the adhesive between Bert and me, but at this time, I questioned if Bert and I had any love for each other at all. I began to question whether Bert and I should remain together and wondered if Bert was capable of expressing positive emotions.

I began to want Aubrey to know that Bert raped me and made me pregnant. I never allowed Aubrey a choice in deciding how he wanted to handle the situation. I sought advice from the women about counseling, but they advised against it because if Bert found out, he would be embarrassed that he can't control his house. These women questioned my relationship with Bert and wanted to know if we were in love because love makes us less lonely, not more so.

Love and Closeness

Speaking with these experienced women became therapeutic for me, and I began to understand so many things. Could people be married and still not be close? I realized Bert and I never developed closeness in our relationship, and that was why I felt so lonely. I assessed my relationship with Bert and realized that he made it difficult to get close to him. I never felt we both understood each other, or that Bert ever took my life goals and dreams seriously. Bert never behaved in a way that I was able to relate to, and because of this, I withheld significant parts of myself from him. Looking back on my relationship with Bert, I never felt he ever considered me a priority in his life or in our relationship. Bert never showed any excitement for any achievement of mine or when noticeably good things happened for me.

Together but Lonely

Many of us believe that if we feel lonely, we are searching for love. We think love is the most profound feeling because it should be the glue that holds us together. Love is the greatest joy we can experience. This may be true under the right circumstances, like being in a relationship and being transparent, naked, and honest with our spouse. We can fall in love with someone who is in love with us and desires the same things we desire. But sometimes it is not love but infatuation that draws people together, and most times, the infatuation is sexual in nature. Sometimes we may love someone, and this person does not love us back or does not love us the way we feel we should be loved. When this happens, much bitterness lives in the person's emotions and thoughts.

I felt Bert was incapable of loving me, and for a long time, it seemed his idea of love was simply to control me. He did not express affection or emotions when I was in pain or received sad and disturbing news. I tried to love Bert on so many occasions, but he made it so hard for me to be open, transparent, and honest with him. I was still so much in love with Aubrey, and I began to realize with more clarity each day that Bert was the wrong person to marry. This was felt even stronger when I remembered what he put me through.

Unhappy in Marriage

Bert and I were living in the same house and sleeping in the same bed, yet I was disconnected from him. This made me assess our relationship, and one thing that became apparent was that we were not close, and I began to wonder if we could ever get close. I met people who appeared to be close with each other event though they were not in love. Bert never cared about the things I cared about, nor did we help each other to care about each other.

This made me wonder, why did I agree to marry him? Is it because of the rape and embarrassment, or was it something else? I remembered I was beginning to feel lonely, and somehow, I thought I would become less lonely by marrying him, but after all these years, I began to realize I was lonelier than ever because we were still not close. Bert sometimes told me he loved me, but I didn't see that love demonstrated, and we never discussed anything or shared any intimacy. I felt he never took time to understand me or care about my goals, dreams, or aspirations. I heard him praising his friends' wives for doing the things I did. He took me for granted. He asked other people for advice. He would take advice from his parents back in Guyana and then expect me to go along with them. In the past, I would get so angry, and we would argue about this, but he would excuse it and continue the behavior, so I grew tired of the disagreements and said nothing more about it.

We grew apart, and I knew I was not his priority. I was unable to relate to him and him to me, and I still had not found the courage to let him know about Martha. I never thought anyone could be so unhappy in any relationship like I was. Maybe this unhappiness was only in my relationship, or maybe I was expecting too much from Bert.

Ways Loneliness Impacted Me

Due to loneliness, my emotions created lots of anguish and caused problems with eating, sleeping, and mood. Some days I could feel the depression so intensely, and I suffered from flu and colds. My last visit to the doctor revealed a depressed immune system, lots of anxiety, perception distortion, and inflammatory problems. My selfworth was dwindling, and my self-confidence was so low, I found myself crying for no reason and talking myself out of wanting to be with the women in my community.

How Loneliness Impacted My Relationships

I found myself thinking these women might be talking about me by using the information I shared with them, and maybe they were even laughing at me. I didn't know what to think or believe. I was hesitant to continue the relationship with these women, and I didn't want to bother with anyone. Sometimes when the women came to the door, I had no desire to answer it because I felt they didn't care about my situation. I was less interested in being with them, and I came up with excuses to avoid them because maybe they were not as committed or interested in me. I was focused on simply preventing myself from experiencing any additional emotional hurt. ***Is It Possible to Be Lonely in Marriage?***

I was lonely prior to marriage, and I was sure that after marriage, I would never be lonely because Bert would keep his promise. How wrong I was because I was so lonely with lots of responsibilities and in a strange country with a detached husband. The quality of my relationship with Bert became poor, and only our children kept me grounded. I tried to determine when this loneliness began. We drifted apart and became disconnected. We didn't even listen to the same music or watch the same television shows, and I couldn't recall the last time we did anything together as a family. I would not miss him or the loneliness when I eventually left. I knew I would find a way to get up and out of here while I still could.

What Is Love?

I heard love explained once as when a man or woman's physical desire is strong for each other, and this person is always on their mind. You think about this person during each waking hour and feel you can't live without this person. The dictionary explains love this way: a strong feeling of affection or attraction that includes sexual desires due to a romantic relationship. The Bible talks about four kinds of love. First there is Eros, known as erotic love. This love is physical, dominated by sexual love or desire, the kind of love between a husband and wife. Next is Philia, which means the close friendship we share with friends. Many times we say to our friends, "I love you," but there is nothing sexual. Another kind of love is Storge, and this is the kind of love we share with our family. It's a bond among mothers, fathers, and siblings. The Agape love is a selfless, sacrificial, unconditional love—the highest of the four types of love in the Bible. I can love my enemies or demonstrate love to people or make sacrifices to people and mean it.

In the New International Version of the Bible in 1 Corinthians 13:4–7, this is how love is explained:

> Love is patient, love is kind. It does not envy, it does not boast, it is not proud. It does not dishonor others, it is not self-seeking, it is not easily angered, it keeps no record of wrongs. Love does not delight in evil but rejoices with the truth. It always protects, always trusts, always hopes, always perseveres.

In the NKJV of the Bible, God states in 1 John 4:7–11,

> Beloved, let us love one another, for love is of God; and everyone who loves is born of God and knows God. He who does not love does not know God, for God is love. In this the love of God was manifested toward us, that God sent His only begotten Son into the world, that we might live through Him. In this is love, not that we loved God, but that He love us and sent His son to be the propitiation for our sins. Beloved, if God so loved us, we also ought

to love one another. God shows us He is love because He gave us His only begotten son. In the NKJV in the book of John 3:16, we read,

For God so loved the world that He gave His only begotten Son, that whoever believes in Him should not perish but have everlasting life.

My challenge was why was I allowing myself to perish in this loveless marriage? Who do I believe in? Was it Bert, my husband, taking me to a place of perishing, or was it what God says in His Word—to believe in Jesus Christ for everlasting life? It became so clear that changes were necessary and fast so that I could live a glorious life here on earth and beyond.

Married for the Wrong Reason

I knew before I married Bert he wasn't my knight in shining armor, nor was he my Mr. Right. I did not consult with the Holy Spirit about this marriage. My motives were wrong for marrying Bert. When I married Bert, it was because of the savage rape and the embarrassment of losing my virginity and getting pregnant with Martha, our daughter. I still had not told Martha or Bert that we were her parents because my parents forced me to terminate my rights as her mother. My mother pressured the midwife, who got paid to forge my parents' signature on her birth certificate. My parents threatened to abandon me and throw me out of their house if I did not allow them to place their names on the birth certificate and never mentioned they are not her biological parents. I was forced to go along with my parents' request because I had nowhere else to go.

Marrying for Selfish Reasons

Many people marry and feel they found their Mr. Right, but neglected to consult the Holy Spirit prior to exchanging their vows. We often see them experience issues that result in trials, tribulations, anguish, disasters, and, many times, birthing children who are exposed to all kinds of neglect and possible abuse. My advice is for us to first assess why we want to get married in general, and why do we want to marry this person in particular. We need to consult with the Holy Spirit by bringing our petition of marriage, then waiting for His response. We must evaluate our motives for getting married, period. Instead of fantasizing and making this person what we want him to be, we need to seek the truth through God. Many times this person may say the right things, do the right things, look and feel good to us, but is this person's characteristics in line with our assignment from God?

Sometimes we feel that because our peers are getting married and having children, we want to as well, yet many times we did not prepare ourselves for parenthood. The relationship we forced upon ourselves, we end up despising, criticizing, and running from because we never sought the Holy Spirit or waited for instructions from God. Sometimes when we get the revelation and discern our marriage is failing, we resort to praying and asking God to change our spouse's behavior. We need to ask ourselves, did God join us in the first place?

Why Did I Get Married?

I remembered when Bert and I started dating. Bert wasn't my gift from the Holy Spirit because we had a disturbing past. However, I let my guard down because my parents and family felt he was a changed person. My parents knew Bert raped me and that Martha is my daughter, but the other family was not privy to this information. I was not convinced Bert is a gift from the Holy Spirit because I suffered in the past with him and saw his inappropriate behaviors toward others and me. He was so different from all his friends. He pretended to be a provider, but provided only the basic needs. He did not protect us from his violent rages. Bert and I argued because we disagreed, and for him, things always had to be his way. Sometimes I questioned how I felt about him and often wondered why I was still with him. I didn't want to be alone, but being with him was hell.

The idea of having a family of my own was what I really wanted. I felt having a husband and children would replace the loneliness. In deciding to marry Bert, I thought I could rely on him when I needed to, but I was wrong. For the first time, I realized we were not in love, nor were we even in a relationship.

Married but Separated

We stopped sleeping in the same bed. Bert usually came home late and drunk and picked fights and arguments, waking the family up and causing all kinds of discord in the household. Bert was stingy and wanted to provide a limited amount of money to cover the household expenses. I prayed daily to God to change my husband's inappropriate behaviors and to make him more responsible as a father and husband. Bert continued to drink, and his abuse became worse. He used profanity and physical assaults. He grabbed things out of my hands and pushed me out of his way. I prayed God would keep my children and me safe.

I didn't love Bert, and I didn't know how long I could tolerate this marriage. Bert never changed his abusive behaviors, nor did he stop his drinking or coming in late at night picking fights with me. I began to stay out of his way and pretended to be asleep before he came home to avoid any confrontations with him. Many times he would wake me up to either ask questions or to get his physical needs met. I used any tactic to come up with excuses, but he did not listen, only reminding me about my duties as his wife. Frustration became my first name because I chose not to smell his alcohol or hear his profanity. I began to feel bitterness toward Bert and had so many unanswered questions running through my mind I knew only God could answer. I prayed to God for forgiveness, and I know God answered my prayers, but I still had to deal with Bert's abusive behaviors.

Marriage with Bert for the wrong reasons caused all kinds of disturbances in my life, and I knew this union was not entered with God's blessings. I understand my actions in marrying Bert resulted in making a mockery of the marriage union.

Home at Last

Our son, Bert Junior, was finally discharged, older and stronger. This was an unbelievable and incredible time for his sister Angelica and me. She loved being with her baby brother, reading to him and drawing pictures for him and sharing stories with him. These were happy and sad moments for me because Bert continued with his late-night rendezvous with his intoxication and coming home when the bars closed. I tried not to allow myself to be distracted with Bert's behavior, and having my children near me gave me lots of fulfillment and joy. I spent lots of time engaging our baby and playing catch-up for the missing time he was hospitalized.

My plan for my children was to enroll them in a school so they could interact with their peers when I returned to work. Bert Junior was making nice progress in all areas of his development. I worked harder now but was not complaining. Our baby stopped all medications, and his specialist and pediatrician visits were now stabilized to normal visits. These were happy times for me, and I stopped complaining to Bert because I realized I couldn't change him—only the Holy Spirit could.

Staying Married for the Wrong Reasons

The institution of marriage was designed to benefit both Bert's and my life with secure loving feelings that would support both of us. Marriage is meant to set a foundation for children and spouses, or so I thought. I became so disappointed that our marriage was not meeting this standard and was so unhappy about our failures. Many of my peers got married before us, and they were divorced for one or many reasons. I refused to stay in this unhappy marriage. I felt staying in this marriage was hopeless because I was so unhappy, and I felt Bert and I lost the vision and commitment of why we got married in the first place. The marriage was dull and becoming depressing. My only fear of divorcing Bert was each of us fighting for full custody of our children.

Fear of Sharing

I heard it said fear is false evidence appearing real. But I wasn't sure this was false evidence because I was becoming more afraid of Bert's behavior. He came home late and intoxicated, and when he was not intoxicated, he lost his temper and used profanity, calling me all kinds of b- and f- words. Bert would rush toward me and hit me with his shoulders while glaring and grimacing at me. Other times he intimidated me by walking into me and causing me to fall, smacking me across my face, or yanking my hair. I tried not to let him see me cry or in pain. I would yell and scream for him to stop, but this empowered him, and he continued to assault me. Now when I anticipated he would assault me, I would move out of his way, or I wouldn't move at all until I was sure of where he was walking to prevent him from hurting me.

I shifted my focus to improving my relationship with my children by interacting with them more. I tried several times to assess why I was staying in this abusive relationship. Sometimes I felt angry and stuck in this hopeless marriage, and I recognized I needed to be unstuck and to create a healthier relationship as I moved forward. I was unhappy, and I deserved happiness and contentment in my own life. I couldn't allow my children to stay in this unhealthy family either. Their self-esteem would suffer, and situations would become unsafe for them.

I overheard a mother saying once that though she's suffering abuse by her husband, she had to stay because she wants her children to live with their father in their lives. I refused to stay in this abusive marriage because of my children, and so I needed my own money.

Creating Self-Sufficiency

I did my best to not say or do things to upset Bert. I became the best wife and worked to keep my house spic and span with meals always ready. I made sure our children were on their best behavior. I made sure that our home environment was peaceful when Bert was home. I urged him to return to our bed. I tried not to argue or respond in any negative way when he was nasty and abusive toward me. Our children were doing well, and I went along with the pretense. I did my best to become the perfect wife. I encouraged Bert to let us move closer to the city, telling him of the benefits for him living closer to his job and what this would mean for him.

Bert was convinced, and we found a home in the city less than fifteen minutes from his job. We moved into this home, and I became the ideal wife and mother. I made sure I exceeded Bert's needs. I kept our home and children beautiful. I shared with Bert the importance of having our children socializing with peers their ages, and I explained the benefits of what this would mean. I convinced Bert that our children should become enrolled in day care and in the elementary public school. Our children did well interacting with their peers, and Angelica was above her peers academically. She came home with lots of stars and awards from her teachers. I reminded Bert of the importance of me getting a job because otherwise, I would lose my teaching license.

I found an administrative job facilitating and teaching teachers. I speak English, Portuguese, and Spanish very well. I felt so blessed to be making money and meeting new people at work and learning the professional culture. I felt good. With the extra money, I was able to contribute to our home, and I opened a savings account at the local bank unbeknownst to Bert. I did let Bert know about the account I had created with my payroll department.

Negative Shift

After working on this job for less than a year, I became involved in two different activities at work, and they provided after-school services for my children with meals. My children made friends, and this opportunity allowed me to use and develop skills in facilitating learning for the teachers and administrators at school. Things developed well for me, and I made many friends with colleagues and in women's groups.

Bert was unhappy with this arrangement and began to torment me daily about quitting this job because it was taking away from his time with the family. I refused and argued, "You are not home until late, and this gives our children an opportunity to learn from other children and to develop interactive skills with their peers."

Bert and I argued, and he began to assault me, hitting, slapping, shoving me anytime he would bring up his demand that I quit, and I refused. He threatened me that if I didn't hand in my notice to quit, he would call and follow up with a visit to the school to speak with the principal, telling him I had to quit. I refused to listen to him. Bert called the school and harassed the secretary to speak with me, and when I was unavailable, he would become enraged. He continued to increase his calls to speak with me. Administrators discussed his harassment, and when he threatened the staff, they called the police, and I was dismissed along with my children. Embarrassed and devastated for the loss of this wonderful position and opportunity for my children, I wept.

I found another job with great benefits and pay, but it lasted only a short time because Bert called and harassed the staff, wanting to constantly speak with me. Again he showed up and cursed, screamed, and intimidated the staff, which resulted in calls for the police again, and again I was let go.

These were some painful and frightening times for my children and me because his abusive behaviors intensified. He would attack me in the presence of our children, and they would jump and run toward me to protect me from being dragged or from objects being thrown at me. Our lives, relationships, health, peace, and this marriage were falling apart. I looked at Bert and felt I no longer recognized this man. My children and I became petrified of him. He demanded to know about my finances, but I pretended not to understand what he was talking about.

I found another job, but this time I did not involve myself in any extracurricular activities. I went from work to home and made an oath not to argue or involve myself in any confrontations with him. I was planning an escape back to my native land and kept this only between God and myself. Not even my children were aware of my plans.

In the Eyes of a Child

Our eyes are the windows of our souls. Our eyes allow us to see and also to envision what we want our lives to become by using our thoughts to align with the Word of God. Many times we focus on the facts that should help us navigate life's journey. But the truth that is written in God's Word is what we must meditate on day and night because this is what will impact our lives in positive ways. However, as parents, we don't always align our activities with God's truth because the facts can become so overwhelming that we fight for the territories of our thoughts, and many times, this does not work the way we want it to. Needless to say, when we don't take the appropriate actions at the right times and seasons, we add stress.

In my life, I experienced many twists and turns, like the number 8. While I was overwhelmed by a toxic relationship with my spouse, I allowed my children to become susceptible to the abuse in my marriage. This placed my children's and my life in imminent danger. I needed to listen to how my children were affected by the poor decisions and choices I made in the name of wanting my kids to live with their father. As parents, when we are being abused and going through pain, hurt, and humiliation, we can be so entranced in the process that we don't realize our children are aware and internalizing our every physical, verbal, economical, and emotional abuse.

What Children See

Our children can see and feel our every abuse and the pain and the visual scars we try so hard to conceal from them. Our abuse casts lots of fear in our children. They fear for our safety, which resonates as anger and disconnect in our children's mind and spirit toward the abuser and even to those who are being abused. This results in a level of distrust in the relationship between our children and us. Many times I have heard mothers say they stay in an unhappy marriage because of their children. Many parents say they don't want their children to grow up without a father because their fathers were not in their lives. However, when our environments prove to be unsafe due to domestic violence, everyone suffers. When domestic violence prevails and makes the environment unsafe, we should leave when the opportunity presents itself. Our children should not live in violent environments because their parents decide to stay for their sake. Sometimes children grow up to repeat the behavior, and it becomes a cycle.

Remember, children will grow up to become adults, and if a young girl is only accustomed to abusive environments, the message to her is that this is acceptable or even to be expected because her mother stayed with an abusive man. This young girl will grow into an adult with children of her own, and she may either abuse her spouse or allow him to abuse her, and the cycle repeats itself because now she and her children are caught in a new but still violent environment.

Abuse is not new to my family or community. My aunts and cousins were beaten with weapons and fists and made bloody, but they still stayed with their husbands because they felt it's an honor to their wedding vows of "till death do us part."

I am angry that Bert raped me and disrupted my life and that he was not held accountable by my parents. When I told them he raped me, took my virginity, and made me pregnant, they still forced me to marry him. Sometimes I would feel it didn't matter if I were unhappy, but I couldn't bear the thought that my children were unhappy. I needed to protect my children in the moment and for their future. I refused to allow my children to be hurt or to experience emotional mishap, triggering disturbances in school, home, and in the community.

My daughter shared with me that her friend's mother was being beaten and the father cursed her mother, and this all made her afraid and sad, and she now cries a lot in school. Her friend does not know if her mother is beaten or hurt while she is not there to protect her mother. Her friend also shared she is most worried her father may hurt her mother permanently or kill her, and she would blame herself because she wasn't there to help her mother.

The Forbidden Talk

My children questioned me about my relationship with their father, and they demanded straight-up answers. They asked me about the screaming coming from my room; they wanted to know why their father pushed, slapped, punched, and pulled my hair and why he cursed at me. My daughter said her father was changing into a bad man who beat up on his wife, and she did not like this because it made her angry when she knew I was being hurt. Angelica said she knows when I cry because my eyes and face are red and swollen.

Angelica and I had a conversation in which I tried to protect her from the harshest truths, but I believed she needed to know the basics because my abuse could no longer be concealed. My daughter remarked that she saw her father changing when he began to curse, smack, shove, and pull my hair, and she heard him warn me about friends and knew he was no longer coming home at a certain time from work like before. She mentioned she saw how his behavior was different in a bad way and that he was often drunk when he came home. He screamed, cursed, and attacked me by throwing objects at me, or rushing up to me and knocking me down. She said many times she saw me running out of his way because I would get hurt if I didn't.

She was angry at her father's bad behaviors and also angry with me for lying to her and staying with him because all he did was hurt me. She shared that this all made her angry, and she felt alone because she didn't know what to do. She was crying alone in her room and had trouble sleeping. She was angry with me for lying to her because she knows her father has been abusing me for a long time. She wanted to know if we were getting a divorce.

I explained to my children that their father and I were having problems. Many families argue and sometimes fight. I didn't know if we would be getting a divorce. I lied because I was planning to get away from him with my children to return to my native country and divorce him. I could see the disbelief in her eyes as well as hurt. This made me feel so bad because I didn't know how to fix my husband's behavior and our relationship. Worse, I now knew my children were aware that I was lying for their father. It bothered me that my Angelica cried in her room when I thought she was asleep. I don't want my daughters to think that all men do is abuse women. I cannot bear the thought that Bert Junior should think it is good to be abusive. He has demonstrated abusive behaviors when he can't get his way with his sister. He would curse, hit, or throw objects like his father. I felt so ashamed, hurt, and betrayed by Bert, and now I no longer could cover up for his abusive behaviors.

I tried to distract myself from the pain this conversation brought, but I could still see the hurt and pain in their eyes. My sustained abuse had a negative impact on my children, though it affected them in different ways. I needed to prepare my children for how to stay safe in the event we had to move or should something happen to separate us.

Back to Reality

Bert stands over me with his hands fisted, yelling that I caused him to beat me up because I did not come when he called me, and he reminds me he will not tolerate disrespect from me. My kids are screaming, "Leave my mommy alone!"

Bert grabs both of them and shoves them in the direction of the stairs, yelling, "Get upstairs!"

Our daughter screams, "I'm not going anywhere because you hurt my mommy!"

Bert Junior imitates his sister and stomps his feet, screaming, "No! Leave my mommy alone!"

I make a silent oath to myself that my children will no longer be exposed to, or become victims of, domestic violence. This abuse must stop. Bert threatens to take our kids away from me if I ever report him or seek help. I know I should go get medical attention, but I'm so afraid it will make the situation worse and result in losing my children because abuse is acceptable by our society.

I'm noticing some obvious signs—Angelica is complaining about being sick, stomachaches, headaches, and she is more tired and refusing to go to school more than usual. Angelica is now eight, and she's witnessing horrific episodes of her father's vicious abuse toward me, and suddenly, the shock of my past engulfs my thoughts. *Oh God, this is not happening.*

I feel nauseous and anxious as I compose my thoughts. The harder I think of changes to make in my current situation, the stronger the perspiration, and panic increases. These thoughts bring me back to my preadolescence at eight years old. Déjà vu strikes as I recall when my eight-year-old friend Ingrid's father killed her mother.

Flashbacks of the Past

Ingrid was timid, shy, and showed attention deficits. She appeared to be in a fog and spoke only to me and sometimes to the teachers. She trusted me over all the other children. She said her father was a police officer, and her mother was a housewife. We walked daily to and from school, and many times we played together at school. We passed each other in the community, but her father did not allow her to play outside the house.

Ingrid told me her parents were having arguments, and she heard her father cursing and calling her mother all kinds of bad names. Her father would assault her mother when he got angry or drunk. She witnessed her father holding his gun to her mother's head and her mother crying so hard, begging him not to kill her. Ingrid said her mother asked him for a divorce. Her father said if she ever left him, he would kill her. Ingrid said she prayed that the gun wouldn't work, and when he pulled the trigger, it didn't—it jammed. She told me her mother does not say or do anything to make him angry. Her father was always angry, and he kicked, punched, and threw things at her mother. Ingrid said her mother had no money, and she wanted to run away, but she couldn't, so they were both stuck and afraid of her father. Ingrid said she stays in her room crying because she was afraid her father would kill her mother, and no one would be there for her. She doesn't want to stay with her father if he kills her mother because she's afraid he will kill her too. Ingrid said she couldn't share this family secret with anyone else for fear her father would find out. This was her reason for not speaking to anyone else in school because she does not want the secret to slip out. She said if her father finds out she let the secret out, she would get into lots of trouble. She said, "My mother is not allowed to leave the house without his permission."

I promised to protect her secret and protect Ingrid from being bullied by other children. I became worried when Ingrid missed school for one week. I went to her house and peeked into the kitchen, hoping to see her, but instead this weird feeling came over me, and I ran back to my house.

Witnessing Her Mother's Death

One week after standing outside Ingrid's house, I heard the teachers whispering. I worried about Ingrid and her safety. I heard the gossiping women say Ingrid's mother was dead. She was found with third-degree burns all over her body, and the husband denies he had anything to do with it. Ingrid returned to school, and she looked sick and lost lots of weight. She whispered to me that she heard her mother crying and her father beating her mother and cursing. She got out of bed to peep at them, then returned to bed in fear she might be caught. Her mother continued to scream, and she knew she was in pain, making a weird sound and begging her father to stop. She heard her father cursing, hitting her harder and harder. Ingrid said she was petrified and covered her ears, closed her eyes, and placed a pillow on top of her head. Ingrid said when she got up in the morning, the house smelled of smoke, and her mother was dead, her body burnt beyond recognition. Ingrid vanished soon after, and I never saw her again.

Effects of Domestic Violence in My Family

My family suffers from poor health, such as heart issues, gastrointestinal disorders, sleep deprivation, upper respiratory distress, and social-emotional problems, and the doctors ascribe it to the effects of domestic violence. Domestic violence creates havoc in a victim's life and in an abuser's family and their working lives. The effects of domestic violence are far-reaching, including detrimental effects on children. Domestic violence causes misery, anxiety, fear, shame, physical and emotional pain, disconnection, displacement, relocation, loss of hope and desires, depression, and financial burdens due to missed work, medical bills, psychological treatment, and in many instances, spiritual, emotional, and physical death.

Effects of Domestic Violence on My Children

My children are victims of domestic violence, and they are suffering from anxiety, emotional distress, sleep disturbances, depression, and problems with eating and with digestion. Remembering Ingrid, my friend who shared with me at age eight that her father took her mother away from her family and friends to live in the country, I couldn't help but think of myself. Ingrid witnessed her mother crying many times. Her mother said she was lonely. Her mother was not allowed to work, nor did she have any friends. She depended upon her father for all financial resources.

Bert is abusing me while our children are experiencing the effects of this abuse. I am hurting; they are also hurting. Our children feel guilty they can't protect me and worry they cause the strife between Bert and I. My children experience neglect, while I experience trauma because I can't attend to their needs or give them emotional support. My children experience confusion when they see me being pushed and yelled at, and they become fearful and ashamed.

I witness my son displaying abusive behaviors when he hurts his sister because this is what he sees his father do to me. One of the major concerns with Bert Junior is that he is developing emotional problems. When my son is not allowed to get his way, he cries or becomes withdrawn and isolates himself. His biggest problem is sharing and making friends as well as being friendly with his sister. Bert Junior has a violent streak and uses aggression toward his sister to get his way. He complains a lot of headaches, stomach pains, problems sleeping, behavior problems, and bed wetting at least three times a week.

Assessing My Relationship

I need to take time to understand and assess where I am in my life, as a mother, and in this marriage. I have been abused for so long that I have become numb to it and have become enslaved to my senses, which rule my spirit and my emotions. God made me ruler over my spirit and my emotions. Therefore, I must leave this relationship for my own safety because if I'm not safe, I can't protect my children. But what happens if Bert finds us if we leave? I need a way to get out of this country and return to Guyana because I know my children and I will be safe there. Also, it has been years since I saw my first daughter, Martha, and she must know the truth about who her parents are. I need to show my children that not all men are abusive and to teach them what to accept and what not to accept. Understanding the attributes of a healthy relationship will build my self-confidence and self-esteem to help other suffering women trapped in the misery of abuse. I want to feel and to be safe again. I need support and information about services and to find someone who will help me. It is important for me to know, understand, and demonstrate healthy and unhealthy relationships to prevent another abusive relationship.

Spiritual Abuse

I've attended many churches from a young age, and issues of domestic violence aren't mentioned there. Many churches don't acknowledge the real issues that plague the congregations and Christians in the community. The churches talk about loving your neighbor as you love yourself, but spiritual abuse is an issue none of the churches address, and it continues to be an ignored epidemic. Pastors behave as though this topic is taboo. The time is now for all church leaders to become educated about domestic violence and the spiritual abuse that is rampant in churches and wreaking havoc in the lives of church members and guests.

Pastors cannot ignore any of the abuses in their churches, including spiritual abuse, because this must be confronted for true connection with God. Many different abuses exist, and although spiritual abuse is subtle and as painful as the other abuses, it also falls under the umbrella of spirituality. Many pastors abuse their authority in many ways. Some of these abuses are demonstrated when members are embarrassed, criticized for leaving the ministry, or made to feel ashamed because they did not meet expectations set by pastors. I witnessed apostles criticize and reprimand members for not following through on assignments. When members attempt to explain, they are silenced and not allowed to speak.

My attendance became mandatory at a meeting. The apostle reprimanded me, and as I began to verify what he was saying, he tried to shut me up and say that I was disrespectful. The apostle and his wife said, "God said, 'Touch not my anointed one and do my prophet no harm.'"

I interjected, "Yes, God said touch not my anointed one and do my prophet no harm, and yes, I'm also a prophetess of God, and you are being warned not to do me any harm. For God rebuked kings for His prophet's sake."

They both looked at me blankly, and I told them I would not tolerate their spiritual abuse because I know what the Word of God says concerning my life.

Many church members and Christians are abused in many denominations, and they are afraid to admit they are being abused by their church leaders because they are made to believe God only speaks to the leaders and will never speak to them because of their sin. Many Christians stay in churches because their families went to the same church or because these churches are in their neighborhood. Some are accustomed to the spiritual abuse and are blind to the feelings of harm rather than healing through their church leaders. Other Christians are so beaten down by the abuse of their pastors, they are numb to its effect. Others leave the fellowship of the saints and lose their faith in churches and pastors.

Many pastors prohibit sinful actions of Christians based on their standards rather than the Word of God. Spiritual abuse occurs when a church or ecclesiastical leader or designee manipulates or dominates people with mind-control tactics. The mind control of many Christians stems from their fear, which is used against them. Spiritual abuses include leaders of churches or their designated authority structure and cults that use manipulation to control its members. It can be difficult for members to decipher when their spiritual leaders are abusing them because these leaders hide their abusive behaviors behind spiritual deception or in the name of God. Many spiritual leaders talk about God, and their members never stop to question them about the God they are referring to. So many female clergy are barred from gracing the pulpit because male clergy feel a woman should never become a pastor over God's people. Therefore, these female vessels never flow into the areas their anointing was destined to reach.

Chosen by God but Rejected by Man

Many male church leaders frown upon ordained female leaders. They see female clergy as inferior to men and neglect to promote these female leaders to deliver God's messages or to lead God's people. Many female leaders are kept in positions that prevent them from standing before the congregation to deliver the Word of the Lord. Women who are anointed by God sometimes lose their focus of whose voice they should listen to and become distracted because they feel they must be in agreement with a pastor. Many times these anointed women see their promotion as coming solely from the pastor, and they would do whatever is required to please him, even disobeying the instructions of God.

God removed me from a ministry because the leader had established his rule that he does not allow God's ordained female servants to speak for two years after ordinance but to volunteer services to his congregation, and then he would decide when I should leave to start the assignment God had instructed me to do. The funny thing about this is I never saw those instructions in God's Word. Therefore, as sons and daughters of the most-high God, we need to seek God now more than ever before. We are led astray because congregants listen only to their pastors and do not seek God through His Word. God told us to study to show ourselves approved, and this biblical mandate comes first because God holds us accountable for our lives, not our pastors.

Judgments in God's House

Leaders need to remember, God said in His Word that judgments would first start in the house of the Lord. The time is now more so than ever when God will hold His clergy accountable for their unacceptable behaviors. God makes a public spectacle of their nastiness if they continue to perform in secret the wrongdoings they thought they could get away with. These leaders are given time to repent and to turn from their wicked ways, but too many feel they can continue with their abusive behaviors because they don't see any immediate physical retribution. But these abuses will end. God will not allow them to abuse their authority while endangering His people any longer. Many church leaders are being exposed for their abusive behaviors.

God is doing a new thing in His churches. As God stated in His Holy Book, He would build His church upon this rock, and the gates of Hades will not prevail against it. Many church leaders ignored God's word and did not realize God built His church upon Himself. God is the rock upon which everything is built, and if a clergy decides to take a Bible and go build a church that God does not approve, it will be destroyed, period.

Spiritual abuse makes headlines. Some church leaders coerced members into situations that resulted in people becoming victims of abuse, in turn stripping them of their innocence. This problem is spreading as more people are falling victim to this system, and it is continuing because the consequences are not stiff enough to match the crimes these leaders are committing. Therefore, these leaders continue to abuse their spiritual authority while destroying the bond of trust with their congregations. Many members of churches only feel confident to discuss their personal issues or domestic problems, abuse, or violence with a church leader. Much of the counsel these leaders provide causes more chaos and divides members or leads to further abuse. This counsel given to His people doesn't glorify God, and God's people become disappointed in the church, detaching themselves from the fellowship of the saints and shepherds of the houses.

Church leaders can be abusive themselves. Abuse includes sexual assault, abusing their wives, keeping multiple partners, infecting their congregation with transmitted diseases, stealing the tithe and offering, and on and on.

Spiritual Abuse by Church Leaders

God said we are not only to be hearers of His Word but doers also. Many ministries are being exposed for their abuse, and many of these ministries will fold because the spiritual leaders thought they were above reproach and can abuse children when God said to suffer the little children to come to Him, not these spiritual leaders. Many pastors preach God's Word, but take God out of His Word. In the times we live in, we see some churchgoers attend church to see the pastors instead of to hear the Word of God. Many pastors do not take a firm stand to address abuse in their churches but instead make excuses about the pressures men go through.

Listen, God can't be mocked, so God began to demote these pastors and expose their hearts, behaviors, secrets, and abuse and now is judging them based on the neglect of educating His people who were sent to these churches to gain wisdom about the Kingdom of God. For any pastor who escapes public exposure of his wrongdoings in this life, God will be sure to distribute His justice in the afterlife.

Spiritual Abuse in Education

In many of the education facilities, politicians and education leaders continue to abuse their authority entrusted to them to carry out the assignment while serving God's people. Many of them serve themselves based on greed. Others create programs and rezoning to academically enslave students they consider to be the least to excel according to the education status quo they finagle. They create many barriers to keep certain ethnic groups from excelling in education and from being prepared to compete in the job markets.

Spiritual Abuse in Businesses

Businesses are not exempt from accusations of abuse. Their cruel policies destroy relationships among families in certain ethnic groups. The media and streets parent children because many businesses continue to get away with offering only minimum wages, which cause families and especially single women to work more than one job. These business leaders revel in their ignorance that God placed them in these assignments to train, lead, and share resources with His people while preparing them. So many female and minority employees are harassed on these jobs and are barred from promotion because they refuse to commit fraud or because these companies would rather promote Caucasian employees who are often less educated or less qualified.

I have been blackballed from jobs because I refused to commit fraudulent acts to expose many clients' records in mental health. I told the boss to do it himself. I know the God I serve promotes me through no man. This man fired me and reported me to the state, but he forgot the God of heaven and earth is also my judge, and He vindicated me. Not long after, the state shut his business down, and he had to go back to being an employee at someone else's business. God is a just God.

Women Lack Spiritual Understanding

I also believe when women don't know or understand our purpose for our own lives, we will live a life of lack, confusion, helplessness, and despair. We leave ourselves wide open for abuse because we allow unqualified men to make decisions for us, and these men abuse us because they don't understand their own purpose. Therefore, women get what we don't expect because until we know who we are according to God's Word, we will continue to stay in the abuse and accept what we don't need or desire. Some of the men women attract don't understand their assignment and are too pompous to recognize they need help, and they don't ask for help even if they do recognize their need because they feel it is not manly.

Wait on the Lord

In addition, many women live meaningless lives because they refuse to wait on God for their husbands but would rather grab a man who speaks sweet nothings as their friends are getting married, and they feel left behind. So many women waste time looking for a man instead of being obedient to God's Word so that when a man finds a wife, he finds a good woman. What lots of women don't realize when they pick up men due to loneliness instead of waiting for the man God ordained is that they are picking up the wrong man with the wrong anointing. The wrong spirits are attached to these men who are now making a deposit in these women's lives that God did not ordain. Whatsoever we pay mind to in our thoughts, ideas, and feelings will now manifest in our physical world. Our physical world is a manifestation of our mental world.

Because many women don't know the truth of who they are, they begin to look for love and attention and become prey to these men who now project onto the women their feelings of anger. Women succumb and allow unauthorized men to mishandle them. Because both of their lives are unfulfilled because they did not follow God's will, they try to fill the void in their lives. As a result, these men begin to abuse the women. Until men and women begin to come into the revelation of who God says we are, we will not be able to walk in our destiny, and the violence of abuse will continue.

Emotional Abuse by the Clergy

Emotional abuse is more elusive and goes unseen. Often, women don't realize they are being abused because this form of abuse is not physical and leaves no visible bruises. However, emotional abuse can be more damaging to the abuse of self-confidence and self-esteem.

I suffered years of emotional abuse in my family and in my marriage to Bert. I cannot even remember when my abuse and depression began. I experienced years of humiliation and abusive treatments that diminished my sense of self-worth and my identity. This kind of abuse exposed me to all kinds of derogatory language, belittling, shouting, demands and isolation, being yelled at, and being blamed for things and actions I didn't do. Bert felt lots of pleasure in insulting me and causing me such shame and embarrassment. My spiritual life suffered because I was broken with not enough energy to pray, and I abandoned the fellowship of the saints. This made Bert happy, of course.

Verbal Abuse by Pastors

Most women don't understand or recognize when they are being abused. When a boyfriend, partner, or husband calls a woman outside her name, uses put-downs or profanity toward her, this is verbal abuse. Verbal abuse sometimes includes such words as the b——— word, babe, broad, whore, dumb, gal, chick, stupid, good-for nothing, useless, and other such words that are meant to make the woman feel small and ashamed of herself. When pastors give women wrong counsel by emphasizing they stay in a marriage, women's lives can be in imminent danger from verbal and spiritual abuse.

Social Abuse in the Church

Many people are concerned that there be a separation between churches and schools. However, what about the separations within the congregation itself? Many members of churches are not promoted to certain ministries when they are not tithers. The cliques, especially in many of the big churches, do not promote some of these members unless they meet criteria set. Many members are prevented from interacting with the pastor and first lady; other members pay their tithe but are prevented from demonstrating their talents that should be used for edifying the body of Christ.

Reasons Why Women Are Abused Spiritually

I believe that until several things happen, the reasons women are abused spiritually will continue to be the reasons why women will continue to be abused globally. My question is what is the purpose of the church, and what is the church doing about the acts of spiritual abuse and domestic violence plaguing the body of Christ? God is getting ready to judge His body in many ways, and many of these church leaders will be exposed and held accountable. This means the church is the institution God raised up to judge whether spiritual abuse and domestic violence is righteous or unrighteous, not the court system. God's people need to rise up and speak to the unrighteous acts and take authority over the things that are unjust, such as domestic violence, poor business practices, and the stigma of education in the minority population. Until the churches of the nations of the world rise up and globally judge whether these situations are righteous or unrighteous according to the Word of God, these spiritual abuses will continue. The churches of the nations of the world need to understand what is written in the Bible by asking the Holy Spirit to guide them in the truth and the revelation of the Word of God.

Most churches are so quick to tell women the Bible says God does not believe in divorce, while men kill and destroy women all around the world. I believe the church needs to understand God's purpose for churches on earth and do what is right to protect their women and promote justice for all.

God's Purpose for His Churches

The Word of God in Luke 4:18–19 states, "The Spirit of the Lord *is* upon me, because he hath anointed me to preach the gospel to the poor; he hath sent me to heal the brokenhearted, to preach deliverance to the captives, and recovering of sight to the blind, to set at liberty them that are bruised, To preach the acceptable year of the Lord."

What is the message that should be preached to the congregation, to businesses? The church is supposed to teach the Law of God, the message of hope to men, women, children, and families, and to demonstrate the holiness of God, not harbor pastors who are sleeping around and making counsel with what is not written in the Law of God. Not defend business leaders and owners who abuse their assignment and authority. Not look away while the education lawmakers put programs in place to elevate the consciousness of some and minimize the education of others, while underpaying teachers and stripping them of their skills by devaluing their worth without realizing that without teachers, there would be no careers or people to lead. It's time to stop such nonsense.

Being Unproductive Is Disorder

Jesus allowed Moses to give a bill of divorce to the Israelites when they were unproductive and unfruitful. Therefore, why do some churches tell wives to stay in marriages that are unproductive and damaging to their spirituality? In every country in the world, women are hurt, abused, and killed by their spouses. God does not expect leaders to abuse the people they lead. Calling my church for marriage counsel when my life was in imminent danger turned out to be fruitless because I never got help. Instead, I was instructed to pray.

Church Leaders as Mentors

Why aren't the churches playing an active role in fathering or mentoring their men as most men grow up in homes without a father? So many men's fathers didn't understand their role or purpose; therefore, they never transferred the wisdom their sons needed to apply to their own lives. Many pastors need to be educated about what manhood means and also in what being a man of God should look like. Churches need to provide programs to increase the enrollment of men and to educate them so that real men can emerge and take their rightful places in their own lives and be the heads of their homes. Churches need to be held accountable for their positions and missions of their purpose instead of violating their responsibilities. Some of the churches are allowing many injustices to occur because instead of being God's delegated authority on earth, some of these anointed vessels are having inappropriate relationships, whether their male leaders are sleeping around with men and women or having extramarital relationships. This is not God's purpose for His churches in the nations of the world.

Recovering from Spiritual Abuse

Regardless of the abuses we endure, we still must forgive our debtors because we want God to forgive us our debts. Forgiveness is for us so we can move on and begin to do those things God entrusted in us. Feelings of being overwhelmed may occur as we go through the stages of recovery. We may be angry, frustrated, confused, depressed, sad, and sometimes shocked. Some people will also grieve because of symptoms of spiritual abuse. Some victims of spiritual abuse may even feel that God let them down. God said, "If you abide in Me, I would also abide in you." God also said He will never leave you or me, nor would He forsake us.

God never left us. We lost focus and only sought the pastor instead of allowing the Holy Spirit, our teacher, to lead us to the Word of God and to give us the revelation of the Word of God.

Healthy vs. Unhealthy Relationships

I was misled to believe my relationship with Bert was workable because he paid the household bills. I married him, and we were supposed to live happily ever after and somehow pretend to be the perfect couple, but things did not quite work out that way. Marrying Bert was a big mistake, and looking back, I don't know why I thought he was ever going to change.

When my friends and family complained about their spouses belittling them, cursing and abusing them, I didn't see anything wrong with it because since I was a child, I witnessed these behaviors in my family, and they were treated as normal and acceptable. The same husbands who abused their wives also took care of their family needs. Material things were provided for the families during the abuse, and these women never turned their backs on their marriages.

These women were reluctant to complain or to leave their abusive husbands. Instead, they said they believed if their spouses did not love them, they would not beat them. Separating or filing for divorce was not acceptable behavior in my culture. There were times a wife or girlfriend would confide in trusted women about the abuse, but they only wanted to vent. The complaint wasn't about wanting to leave the relationship or having the man leave the house. If it were suggested that the woman should leave and take refuge elsewhere, she would respond to that counsel by never speaking to that person again. Now I realize my view on healthy relationships has been distorted over the years due to what I witnessed in the relationships of my family and friends.

I want a healthy relationship. I did not know a difference existed between a healthy and unhealthy relationship, but I figured it out along the way, and I know what is right. In many of the cultures I'm privileged to be a part of, women are supposed to be seen and not heard. Many women aren't allowed to express concerns or disagreements or to voice or express their thoughts or to share opinions because their opinions don't matter. Many women in my family were treated with disrespect and were told they were second-class citizens. They were not allowed the same privileges as their husbands or the men in the family or community. Poor counsel from family and friends and my own ignorance of what a healthy relationship is all about caused me to spend much of my life in an unhealthy relationship.

Unhealthy Counsel

I became tired of fighting with my parents, and other family and friends kept harping on how I will be an old maid and I should just marry Bert. I was unhappy marrying Bert, and I was unhappy being single. On top of it all, I refused to expose the secret of the rape and losing my virginity, so I saw no other way but to accept my parents' wishes and marry Bert. I felt trapped with no options and therefore agreed to marry Bert. Afterward, I realized we didn't have a close relationship, nor were we in any way connected. All along, I felt this void, and I realized that although he is a warm body in bed, I always feel cold because he isn't a nurturer but a self-centered abuser.

Many women and I share similar stories of loneliness inside a marriage. I still, after all this time, feel barriers and emptiness living with Bert. Understanding healthy or unhealthy relationships is new to me. All my life I saw and heard women being abused in their homes, communities, and on their jobs, and at no time were the abusers held accountable by the legal system. I began to feel such emptiness in my life, but nothing could replace these feelings. I had to change my mind-set so as not to believe the untrue and hurtful things Bert said to me. However, changing my mind did not replace the emptiness I felt. Instead, the new way of thinking distracted me from my assignments and took me off course and left me feeling incomplete, empty, and dissatisfied.

Until one day, by accident, I found what made me happy, made me filled, what gave me peace, gave me confidence and boldness. I found what reassured me. I found a reason to laugh with confidence. I found myself when I understood God's Will for me, and I became passionate about understanding my life's journey and how to invite the Holy Spirit in my life. This revelation began as my secret relationship with my Abba Father, God.

My Secret Relationship with God

I remembered from a young age of two that God showed me things. As I got older, God began to speak with me and to show me visions about things happening to people. Things to come, God would show me. God has always spoken with me. God always kept me well informed about what people were saying about me. God saved me countless times—rape at four and near drowning at six when I wandered away from home and walked to the river. I found a plank and placed one side on the land, and the other side I set in the water. I jumped on the plank, and the next thing I knew, this plank began to drift from the land with me sitting on top as it headed down the river. I was shocked and terrified. God showed me a vision on how to use my feet as a paddle, and this motion caused the plank to drift toward land, and as soon as it got close enough, I jumped on solid ground.

For the first time in my life, I see myself the way God sees me. I decide to spend some quiet time to assess where I am and where I need to be. I begin to seek the Lord day and night. At this point in my life, I realize I need a better relationship with God, and I ask my greatest teacher, the Holy Spirit, to guide me into all truths and to direct my path. My comforter begins to show me how to navigate my life, and things became easier for me.

Multitasking is one of the greatest gifts the Holy Spirit taught me, and many people would ask me how I'm able to do so many things. When I shared the answer—that the Holy Spirit taught me— they did not believe me.

My Greatest Teacher

I communicate with the Holy Spirit in our sacred relationship, which began long before I met Bert. Many people were unaware of this because I never shared it with anyone. Besides school, I am in church at least three times every week—Sunday, Tuesday, and Friday nights. I love being in the presence and fellowship with other saints. I love to hear about the things of God. I developed a hunger and thirst to learn about the life of Jesus Christ. Hearing and reading about what pleases God encouraged me to want to do the right things. I wanted a road map to navigate my life to make sure I'm on the right track. Attending church kept me focused and hungry to return to church each week. I felt strengthened by the Word of God and sharing with the other saints. I'm busy with church activities. I love to sing, to worship, to praise, and to pray.

I wanted a closer relationship with God; therefore, I asked the Holy Spirit to teach me the revelation in God's Word during our times of fellowship. I wanted to become a servant of God; therefore, I began to serve Him by serving His people. I wanted to treat people with love and respect if and when they were not treating me that way. I went into the scriptures to learn how I can love my enemies and people who call themselves my friend. I spent time in the scriptures and learned how to meditate on the Word of God and ask the Holy Spirit to teach me how these scriptures relate to my situation and life. I became so excited about the things of God that attending church and serving God became my joy. I learned how to behave during adverse situations and to look beyond my issues.

Relationship with My Family

The first time I remember feeling emptiness was at two years old. I always tried to fit in with family gatherings. It seemed there were so many things happening around me, but I never felt included, and I know my presence did not matter to my family. As I assess this period of my life, I see I was a bystander, though I was supposed to be part of the family package. As I got older, for me to be noticed by my family, I would serve my family by volunteering to do chores no one else wanted to do because this made me feel useful, and it got their attention. I still felt my family did not acknowledge me as a person and that I did not matter to them. This did not prevent me from fulfilling my family's needs and filling the gaps to complete additional chores around the house and the yard.

We can describe relationships as personal, private, professional, or as a connection or an association. God is also about relationships. Relationships can be ordained; equal yoked, based on assignments, long- or short-term. Many people choose intimate partners based on the amount of money he/she makes, the Ivy League colleges they attended, the job titles they hold, as well as the neighborhoods they live in. But these things are not about equal-yoked relationships. God knows the plans He set aside for each of us, as well as the assignments, skills, goals, vision, abilities, passion, and creativity He placed in us.

Many times if we get into relationships, both professional and personal, in which we are consumed by the demand and discord of the partner, we come to realize that we didn't belong there together. Some people stay in hopes of fixing the relationship and never leave, despite warning signs of serious trouble, and the result is severe discord and sometimes horrific abuse.

We are to remember that if we are without a vision, we will perish and become unfocused. I lost many years of my life in such relationships. I had no goal or plan, so I never wrote down my vision, and I wasted time trying to get someone's approval and permission, only to realize that I need to commit first to my own assignment. In these relationships, I had no written vision and no way to clearly assess who was in my life, why, and what this person is meant to do.

This resulted in my involvement in many unhealthy relationships. For many years I allowed people to call me outside my name and to talk down to me. I was afraid to open my mouth because I felt insecure. I am mindful not to say anything to upset people when they would use derogatory words to describe me or to purposefully hurt my feelings. What I realize now is if I don't like my situation, only I can transform it. The lesson I learned is that many people are only concerned about themselves, with little to no care about anyone else.

Healthy Relationships

In the honeymoon phase of our relationship, Bert and I were able to discuss issues surrounding sex, family, money, career, and education. Our relationship included effective communication and respecting each other's ideas and thoughts. We were honest and fair on issues involving male and female rights, and we expressed equal views and trusted each other—or so I thought.

I believe healthy relationships must be based on respecting each other's ideas and thoughts. Each person must treat each other without any biases. In a healthy relationship, the people involved should be able to make decisions together while discussing the agenda and coming up with solutions to problems.

Unhealthy Relationships

I witnessed my own family members abuse others with deadly weapons. I always wondered why they stayed in these abusive relationships. One such incident I witnessed was with an aunt. This was Christmas week, and my aunt was preparing the mood, making the home festive with decorations. She was preparing her ingredients to make cakes, bread, and other pastries. I remember her meats were waiting to be cooked when I heard her name yelled from outside her house. Unsure of what was happening, panic set in.

Her husband was drunk, yelling her name and charging into the house. My aunt tensed. I didn't know what was happening. My aunt ran through the back door, and her children ran into the bedrooms and hid under the beds and in the closets. I followed them and was so scared, not knowing what would happen next.

Her husband charged through the bedrooms, cursing, screaming, and hitting the beds. I heard the sound of a steel or metal object. When I peeped, I saw a large shiny machete in his hands, and he continued to scream her name, demanding she come out of hiding.

Another time I witnessed my aunt's husband punch her several times in her head, and the force of the punches threw her across the room. Her body hit the wall before she collapsed on the floor. Her body lay lifeless as blood oozed out of her nose and skin. I screamed as her children and I rushed to her to see if she was still alive. It took a while before she responded to us. Her drunken husband stood over her. She began to move her body while opening her eyes, and we continued to scream her name and shake her.

These incidents were a pattern of regular weekly torture of verbal abuse, cursing and calling her names, and physical attacks.

Over the years, I wondered about the relationships I saw in which the man abused the woman. The abuse and torture never stopped, and the women never left. Their children grew up in these abusive households until they were old enough to leave, and now they have continued the abuse in their own families. I grew up thinking this kind of abuse was an expression of love and was normal. That perhaps this is how you know your spouse loves you, by assault and attacks, and that this is how men are supposed to show their love to their wives. I often wondered why women stayed to endure such horrifying abuse. Maybe they worried no other man would want a woman with so many children.

You Get What You Tolerate

Bert has control of any decision involving purchases for the home, money matters, career, and education. He demands I should comply with everything he decides because he is the head of our home. Bert has become unsympathetic about medical concerns, like severe pain during menstrual cycles. He pressures me to have sex when I do not want to or when I am in pain. Bert no longer wants me to spend time with my family or friends. He wants me only to spend time with him, and this always ends in arguments and fighting. He monitors my every move, and I have to check in with him. We could spend hours arguing, and he will throw things at me. I have become his punching bag, and his new name for me is mother f—— or stupid b——. We no longer share the same views on equality for men and women, effective communication no longer exists, and trust and honesty went through the window along with respecting each other's ideas and thoughts.

Bert continues to pressure me about my job. He forces me to quit or gets me fired for one reason or another. He hates me working, and he has become extremely inconsiderate of me as he gains control of my being. Anytime he suspects I have made a friend with anyone or if someone calls me from our neighborhood, he pressures me into moving because he does not trust anyone who would want to be my friend. As he puts it, "She will influence you to make bad decisions." I am exhausted from our many fights and arguments, and I'm constantly walking on eggshells.

Time to Take Action

Being a victim and survivor of domestic violence, witnessing so many women hurt and killed by their abusers, I believe abuse is never acceptable. Someone must answer the call and advocate against abusers and systems that validate this kind of detriment on women. So many women are taught to accept this behavior as a token of these men demonstrating their love. Too many women believe from young ages that if their men did not abuse them, these men did not truly love them. Many women are traumatized by the punches, kicks, burns, miscarriages, and humiliation in the presence of their neighbors, but are made to believe these behaviors are normal because of their marriage vows.

I witnessed this culture in my family and in my community, and I experienced these behaviors in my own life. I know this behavior is wrong. Abuse is not acceptable and should not be allowed. So many mothers have lost their lives, and their children were left with strangers, family members, or systems. Many of these children relocated to my neighborhood, sometimes to work or to live with a friend to clean her house in exchange for a roof over their head. Sometimes this arrangement did not go well, and these children themselves became victims of abuse, including sexual assault or rape, or they were thrown out of the house when they refused to cooperate. Years later, these children's lives were never the same because many of them continued the abuse they sustained, and so they perpetuated the violent cycle, the generational curse and stronghold of many families.

Saved by Grace

I met one of these children who moved into my neighborhood when I was a girl. Her name was Mariah. She was a little older than me, and I observed her walking alone several times daily, never in a hurry. I engaged her in a conversation, and she shared with me that she didn't want to be in the house by herself because her mother's boyfriend touched her private parts, and she feared him. She also said she was so hungry, and her mother went to look for day work. I invited her in and fed her and reassured her that I would make sure she was safe so she could stay at my home until she saw her mother passing by on her way home.

She commented on how my home was beautiful with nice furniture and lots of food. She was so thankful to have a place of safety and with food. She started coming to my home instead of walking the street. One night after my family and I had gone to bed, we heard a loud knock on the door. I jumped out of bed to find my new friend crying. Her clothes were rumpled with missing buttons, and she was grabbing my doorknob as she kept looking over her shoulder as though she were expecting someone. At the door, she pushed past me, and I saw this large figure run toward my door as my friend commanded me to shut it and lock it quickly. The man banged on my door, screaming that my friend's mother left him in charge, and he was supposed to watch her until her mother returned from work. He continued to bang on my door, and my guardian instructed me not to open it.

When Mariah was calm enough to speak, she told me while she was asleep, she was awakened by his weight on top of her. It was her mother's boyfriend, ripping her clothes off and trying to penetrate her with his penis to rape her. She told me she fought so hard and picked up objects next to her bed, hitting him so hard with them until he lost his grip, and she pushed him off from on top of her, and she ran out of the house as fast as she could to my home to safety.

She told me this was not the first time he attempted to rape her. She mentioned she saw him peeping when she was getting dressed. Her bedroom had no door, so he entered whenever he chose.

I am so sad for her that she had to be exposed to such trauma. When we think things are bad, always remember that someone else is having a worse experience. I was thinking my family was poorer than most families I know. However, so many of the people in our community were poorer than my family and were experiencing all kinds of trauma in their own homes. My father was talented, and my mother worked to take care of the family.

Looking back, I know poverty is in the mind because we were created in the likeness and in the image of God, and He is not poor. Unless we change our minds about who and whose we are by not tolerating domestic violence, nothing will change in our lives. We must be the change agents and step out in faith.

Seeds of Blessings

As my thoughts went back to Mariah and how she was able to trust me and find safety in my family's shelter, I realized at a young age, when I did not understand a lot about servanthood by helping Mariah, I have planted powerful seeds in other people's lives. I realized these powerful seeds that I refer to as deeds I have planted are now making room for my own life. It was years ago that those seeds were planted in Mariah's life, and she was kept safe from harm, and those seeds are now making room for my children and my own safety in this foreign land.

I remember my friend Ingrid, the trauma she went through, and the loneliness she felt of living in a new city, and I was the only person she connected to. I am so glad I was able to see and feel her pain and isolation and abuse. I am so glad I was not like the other kids who turned their noses up against her and teased her and bullied her and made her feel unwelcome. I am so glad I planted great seeds in Ingrid's life. She confided in me and felt safe. Despite the abuse she witnessed in her own home, she was in peace in my presence.

The revelation is so profound—years later, I am experiencing what Ingrid felt and what Mariah experienced. God placed people in my life to show me the grace I have bestowed upon these two girls. We have to be careful when people are placed in our presence not to abuse them because we perceive our situation to be better than someone else's. Someone may feel they are better because she has more resources, money, education, or lives in a better neighborhood, but sometimes the future can be unpredictable, and one gets back the same seeds she sows into someone else's life. So we must always sow good seeds and put ourselves in the place of others who may seem the least among us to feel what they may be feeling.

God is no respecter of person. If God can do it for Ingrid and Mariah, I know He can do it for me. God said it is according to my faith, and I have the faith and believe my coworker will help me with the information and connect me with the resources to return to my native land with my children.

Returning to Where It Began

This is the second time I am planning to return home to my native land, though for very different reasons. This time I'm a wife and mother, and I have to return to ensure my children and I are safe before it is too late.

As I process the benefits of returning to Guyana, I realize my resources, including my family and friends and the teaching position I had, were not bad and that I enjoyed those experiences so much compared to where I am at this time of my life.

Never did I imagine I would be running back to my native land to be safe where I know I will be protected, and my children and I will be far from the abuse of Bert we have sustained over the years. Sometimes I feel we have to leave so we can appreciate what we have and for us to discern who is in our life. Leaving Bert is a must for my own well-being and safety for our children and myself because his behaviors are dangerous, and my major concerns are that he would hurt me so badly, it may take me years to recover. I have to leave him for my sake and my children because my children do not deserve his abuse, and I am afraid they could get hurt trying to protect me from his attacks.

Cultural Issues of the Unmarried Mother

During these days, my culture frowns upon unmarried mothers, and I know I will be ostracized when I return to my native country to file for a divorce. Domestic violence in Guyana is treated as a family dispute, and no legal action is taken. But I also know my safety and my children's safety and our well-being are vitally important. Our peace of mind is important, and this also prevents me from staying in this abusive marriage. I know the naysayers will have a lot to say, but because I don't deserve to be abused by anyone, I will find a way to leave this country, return to my own, and file for a divorce. I am not to be blamed for my past, and my present condition is not my fault, but staying in this abusive situation and hindering my future would be my blame and responsibility.

What if he hurts me? What would happen to my children? Now the reality is facing me that not only am I endangering my life, but also the lives of our children. All these years I was living a lie. I wanted this marriage to last for my children's sake. I feel different now because the abuse has become worse, and Bert's physical and emotional attacks on our children and me are out of control. It is now the frequent physical abuse, the rape, and the imminent danger I'm in that concerns me. All these years I made excuses for Bert's physical, emotional, economical, and psychological abuse. I even covered for Bert when he assaulted me. I lied to my family, friends, and coworkers about how I got the many bruises on my body, and I told my family and friends they were from falls or from bumping into furniture or walls. I lied to my family and friends and told them Bert and I have such a healthy and loving relationship because I didn't think these people would understand.

Bert's behavior is worse now, and when he gets in a rage, I don't know the person he becomes. I am so scared; I am becoming numb with the fear Bert inflicts in me. The fear intensifies daily the longer I remain with him. I'm beginning to think if I don't take care of myself and Bert continues to assault me, something terrible may happen to me, and it may be too late. I have to let go of all the promises we made because I haven't seen the realization of these promises, and we haven't had a meaningful relationship in a long time, and maybe we never had. I have been in such turmoil, I lost track of me. I realize the main reason I stayed in this abusive relationship is because I'm longing for Bert to apologize for raping me and telling me how sorry he was.

The reason I overstayed my time in this abusive relationship was because of fear. I became afraid of him and afraid he would take our children and disappear someplace with them, and this was the major reason he was never told that Martha is his daughter. All the dreams and promises I made went to waste, and I was now feeling that nothing worked out as I had planned. I want things to be the way they use to be with Aubrey, but I married Bert and never went to look for Aubrey. Years later, I'm feeling the trauma of marrying Bert the rapist. Would things ever be the same? Over the years, things have become horrible with Bert, and they are only getting worse.

The Importance of Maintaining Focus

To get anywhere in life, we must have goals to follow, not the wrong people to get stuck behind. It's important for me to understand the abuse I witnessed as a child and experienced in my life, but not to accept it. I remember at some points in my relationship with Bert, he would say and do the things he knew I wanted to hear. We would take short trips together, and he would often say things like, "No other relationship did for you what I am doing."

I'm correcting him. The nicest male friend I ever had was Aubrey, but he disappeared, and I never had another male in my life besides Bert, either before or since Aubrey. Anything Bert did he wanted attention for and would get upset if I did not acknowledge and praise what he did. He would not wait for me to comment—he became upset because my response was not automatic.

At one time, I thought I was special in my relationship with Bert. I don't feel that way anymore. When he began his controlling behaviors, I called him out on it. He informed me he was jealous, not controlling.

When he felt he had me hooked and that I would not leave him, the domestic violence began. He would say things to make me think something was wrong with me or confuse or insult me. As time went on, he would become so angry when I would want to talk about things in the relationship, he would tell me how stupid I am. When I would ask him about his behavior, he would continue his profanity or shove me.

In many countries in the world, husbands or boyfriends are still administering domestic violence to their wives or girlfriends without any penalty imposed on them by the legal systems. This validates the behaviors of the abusers; therefore, the abuse continues, and many women have lost their lives in the process. Many mental health professionals have attempted to explain why some men use violence against their wives or girlfriends and other loved ones. Some of these clinicians believe the abuser may be under the influence of one or more of the following: chemical dependency, economic hardship, family dysfunction, lack of spirituality, poor communication skills, provocation, past abuse, witnessing abuse, and stress. While these issues can be associated with the abuse and battering of women, they are not the causes. Abusers use violence to gain control. The abuser receives little consequences if he is sent to jail for a short period or pays a fine. It is not enough of a penalty compared to the abuse inflicted on the woman. Until violence against women is treated as a crime with severe consequences, this horrific damage will continue.

The time for blaming anyone is over because my destiny is in my hands, and I must react and remain alive and in my right mind without any more harm. None of us knows when we first meet someone if he is an abuser until we are involved. What did God intend for us to be, not what society thinks…that is the answer. It is crucial to have a relationship with God so we can hear what His plans are for our lives.

Help Me, Please

I mustered the courage and shared my dilemma with a coworker I considered my friend. She asked, "Why don't you leave Bert?"

My response was, "How do I leave?"

I shared with her that the reason I haven't left this abusive relationship was because of fear and that I wanted my children to be raised in a home with a father. I told her, "I have so many questions, and I have no answers, and I don't know where to begin." I felt over the years that if I obeyed Bert, he would change. He had such a hard life growing up, he told me. His parents were so mean to him. His father beat him and his mother, and sometimes his father locked them out of their house. I was in denial for years and believed Bert loved me and did not mean to beat me up or to call me names.

"He is not always mean," I said to her. "And if I leave him, no one is there to care for him."

She looked at me and said she would help me to leave and to do everything in her power to make sure my children and I were safe. My friend shared with me that she would keep my information in confidence and not share it with anyone. She told me she knew I was being abused, and she saw the same signs with her sister, who was killed by the sister's husband because she wouldn't leave him. Her husband is now serving time in jail, and she is raising her niece and nephew, so the children are motherless and fatherless. This made me weep because the reality of domestic violence does kill people and interrupts the lives of everyone involved.

My friend told me she became an advocate over the years and promised to help anyone coming to her and asking for help. She shared with me that she misses her sister so much, and she can't bring her back, so she does for women in abusive situations what she couldn't do for her sister because her sister no longer had the strength to leave her abusive husband. She told me her sister suffered abuse for many years and was hospitalized from broken ribs, forced abortions, burns, and fractures, but still returned to her husband because she said her husband said he loves her and would not do it again.

This was repeated for all the years they were married until she was killed because his dinner was not ready and served one day when he came home early. My friend told me her sister's body had so many bruises at different stages of healing and iron marks on her back. It looked like he used her back as an ironing board to iron his clothes. Her body was also covered with cigarette burn marks.

Prior to sharing my fear and abuse with my friend, I felt I couldn't tell anyone about what's going on in my house or relationship with Bert. I'm so glad I did, and this made me feel so much better. I have not felt this hopeful in so many years, and I have set my mind on leaving

Bert and this country. I stopped lying to myself about Bert's behavior when he's not in a good mood. I know Bert is cruel and abusive and has been abusing me for many years, and I recognize that I have become immune to his abuse. But after seeing my children's behavior and the effect of the abuse on their lives, staying is not an option. I know Bert has had no consequence from his attacks on me, so his abuse has only gotten worse, and he will never change as long as I stay. I refuse to be a victim any longer, and after speaking with my colleague and friend, I am encouraged to do what I need to do to leave Bert.

Loving Myself

I found the reason to begin loving myself for the first time since the savage rape. It is so hard and unbelievable that I had so much love inside of me. I can't explain the power I feel in loving myself. This love radiates from the deep recesses of my mind, heart, and spirit. It makes me feel so good, and as I begin to read my Bible and meditate on scriptures about love and allow positive thoughts to enter my mind, the fear, numbness, depression, sadness, frustration, and anger dissolve away. Pure love and wellness overtakes me in ways I can't explain. This feeling is like electricity, and it overpowers me and radiates in my body and moves throughout. Peace and wellness overtake me and strengthen me. My thoughts become clear.

Enough Is Enough

Everything I need to travel with has been provided by my coworker, including airfare and transportation. I get up the morning we're traveling, and I take my kids to school and go to work as usual. I had it arranged so that I was leaving work on my break to take my kids to a doctor's appointment, but instead I drive to the airport. I do not need to check in since my documents are there, and they are expecting me. We board the plane, and my children and I never look back, nor do they ever ask me about their father. I refuse to be a statistic; Bert's parents refused to train him up in the ways he should grow. Therefore, I have gotten to a place in my life where my children have become the most important people in my life, and I have to be important as well for them to be safe. I choose not to stay with Bert just to say I have a husband. I realize the pain of staying is much worse than leaving while I am still alive and in my right mind.

Putting My Life Together

I return to my native land, Guyana, South America, and unlike all the feelings of being overwhelmed I had expected from the naysayers, it was quite the opposite. My friend connected me with the school system, and unbeknown to me, I am hired by the superintendent to manage the education department. I am offered an awesome position in the district, overseeing all the principals in the schools. I am well received by my family, friends, and colleagues where I last worked as a facilitator in the school system. I am provided with a free furnished home and free utilities with all free amenities in the community, including recreation facilities and two swimming pools. I am provided with an all-expenses-paid SUV. When I left teaching, I did not realize I had not taken my earned leave time. To my surprise, my earned time was transferred to my new position, so I was able to take two weeks' paid vacation to set up my new home and had time to reconnect with my colleagues and my loved ones.

Both of my children were accepted in the Ivy League schools about five minutes from my office; therefore, I am able to transport them to and from school daily. My children have adjusted well. They are calm, and I see my children smiling again. My children never ask for their father.

First Things First

I had money in both of my savings and checking accounts in Barclays Bank Ltd. in Georgetown, Guyana, and my money had accumulated lots of interest and more money. After interviewing several attorneys, I hire a law firm to handle my divorce and children's custody. Over the many years I was abused and raped, I took pictures and kept a journal, and these I kept in my safe deposit boxes. While I lived abroad, I mailed my documents to my bank to be deposited in my safe deposit boxes. The incidents when Bert abused our children were recorded, and I took my children to their private doctors and had statements written by these doctors. I produced these documents to my attorney, requesting Bert should not have any joint custody of our children. My attorney filed for my divorce with a restraining order, stating Bert should not contact our children or me via text, visits, emails, phone calls, or by showing up at our job, school, dwelling, or any recreational facilities, or he would be arrested.

Next on my agenda is to get my daughter Martha's birth certificate revoked from my parents' names and rewritten to reflect her birth parents. I had to get blood work done, and I had a copy of Bert's birth certificate and his doctor's record with his blood type, which were presented to my attorney. I requested full custody of my firstborn.

While these requests were in process, I asked my attorney to inform my children's school in writing about the restraining order against Bert. One of the most painful meetings to be held was with my parents, my children, and myself. I went into prayer asking God to grant me my heart's desire and to let this meeting be peaceful and according to His plan. I also fasted for twenty-one days prior to selecting the attorney or accepting my new job or setting this meeting.

I believe I was preparing for this meeting for many years, and though I appeared calm, I was panicking inside because I did not know how things would turn out. I believe when God said in His Word that it would be according to my faith if my faith were the size of a mustard seed. My parents agreed to the meeting, but they never asked me what we would be talking about. When I saw my Martha, I longed to hold her, to be a part of her life. I was so excited to see her, and she was excited to see my children and me. Little did she know they are her siblings.

At our meeting, I hid nothing from my children or my parents. I let them know what happened between Bert and I when I was a teenager. I talked about how he abused me, raped me, and took my virginity. I let them know my parents did not support me, but instead they placed me to live in a group home for pregnant teens, and they seldom came to visit me. While living in the home, I was tortured and ridiculed along with the other pregnant teens, and many of the teens were raped in the home. While I was there, I went into a severe depression and spent many days crying. When Martha was born, my parents signed their names to her birth certificate and other documents, and I was not allowed to bond with Martha or spend any time with her while at the home or when I returned to my parents' home, or else they threatened to throw me out of their house while we were living in this foreign country.

My parents looked horrified when I was speaking and tried several times to shut me up, but I insisted this time they will not shut me up because I am stronger, and I am getting Martha back. I let my children know my parents never held Bert responsible for raping or abusing me, but instead years later forced me to marry him to prevent the exposure of the fact that I had a baby born out of wedlock and that I was not a virgin. I told my children the truth about Aubrey and how, when I returned to the city, his letters to me were confiscated, and I never received them nor have I ever laid eyes on him again. Aubrey and I were supposed to get married, and we were saving ourselves for each other. Bert showed up in the country when I ran away from him because I was afraid he would abuse me. I didn't know how Bert knew where I was living, but someone in my family was feeding him information about my whereabouts. I know Bert had something to do with Aubrey's disappearance and me not receiving any of his letters, and after I was raped, I was too embarrassed to let Aubrey know that I had been raped and was also pregnant. I was so embarrassed, afraid of Bert and my parents, and had no one to turn to. I chose not to bother Aubrey about my dilemma because I didn't think Aubrey would want "damaged goods." My relationship with Aubrey ended then, and I never heard or saw him, and I was never able to bring closure to the man who stole my heart.

My mother begins to weep, and when she does speak, she asks for forgiveness. She confirms to Martha that they are not her parents and everything I said was the truth. Martha begins to weep as she runs toward me and grabs me and clings to me, crying on my shoulder. Martha says she always knew and felt a strong bond to me and always wondered why my parents forbade her from having anything to do with me. Martha is introduced to her younger siblings, and they are so excited to have a big sister, and she is excited to have siblings to care for.

My parents share with us that they and Bert set Aubrey up by lying and forging papers, including paying off a lab to say the specimens of Bert's were Aubrey's and that it was Aubrey who raped me and impregnated me. Aubrey was found guilty. He lost his job and was sent to prison for statutory rape of a minor. Aubrey served many years in jail for a crime he didn't commit, and he was released five years ago and came by the house looking for me, but my parents refused to let him know my whereabouts.

My parents present me with Aubrey's unopened letters he wrote me over the years. I weep uncontrollably because for the first time in my life, I realize how wicked people can be, and many times, these people are our own family. I inform my parents I have petitioned the court for my daughter Martha, and I am going to inform my attorney about the new development shared in today's meeting. My mother says she will deny it, and I tell her that because I did not trust her that my attorney has witnessed the entire conversation. I had dialed my attorney's number prior to beginning the meeting today, and he is now listening in on and recording it to present it to the court. My parents call my bluff and grab Martha, saying they changed their minds and would not let her go. A moment later the doorbell rings, and two police officers and secret service men are standing at the door. I tell my parents neither they nor Bert will get away with the crime they committed or the pain they have inflicted on my spirit over the years. I tell my parents I will get a blood test to see if they are even my real parents because good parents would never treat their child the way they treated me.

I take my boxes of Aubrey's mail and all three of my children and leave my parents' home. The police officers take my parents to the police station and reopen Aubrey's case. This is all more than I can handle. My job and my children's school are informed that Bert is not allowed to have any contact with my children.

Martha is now in college, and we spend lots of time together, bringing her up to speed with our lives and what we missed. She is such a beautiful young woman, and she looks like me when I was her age. She and I are looking at pictures of me, and she is shocked when she sees them. She cries out, "Mommy! This picture is the spitting image of me!"

I laugh. "Yes, I know, honey. Pictures don't lie."

My life has become so busy caring for three children and myself. My children get along so well. My lawyer completed my paperwork, including changing Martha's birth certificate and name to her real parents' names. The investigators go to French Guiana and petition the court, and Bert is brought back to Guyana, and the investigation ensues. This part is overwhelming for me, but it must be done.

My divorce is finalized, thank God. Bert is informed about Martha and is shocked. He is introduced to her in a private room with my attorneys and me present, but he is told no contact would be permitted at this time. Martha and I talk about Bert, and she is informed that it is her decision if she wants to see her father when the investigation is over. She wants time to think about it, but says she wants to spend time knowing her siblings and getting to know me more. I love being a mother to my beautiful children, and this brings me peace and happiness beyond words.

After divorcing, most people experience intense loneliness, which can be so painful. I believe I have been so blessed because I am busy with my children and becoming reconnected with my culture and some of my family and friends. I have so much to do, including things I once relied on Bert to do. Some people may get involved in different support groups to fill the void and feelings of loneliness.

For me it was different, though, because all three of my children are involved in many activities in the community, and I am also involved in recreation activities I picked up again when I returned, as well as a thirty-five-plus club I created for men and women to showcase their talents and to network their craft.

At our third get-together, we decide our group is a black-tie affair, and we meet monthly at upscale restaurants or hotels. Each person gets ninety seconds to introduce himself and his business. To my shocking surprise, one of the new members begins to introduce himself as Aubrey. My mouth flies open in total shock and disbelief. Is my mind playing tricks on me? No, this couldn't be! It has been more than twenty years. No way—this couldn't be my Aubrey, the man who stole my heart years ago.

He is not only elegant, but he is fine. He introduces himself as Dr. Aubrey as his eyes burn into mine, never leaving my face. God encouraged me to start this group, and I never asked why.

Move on with Your Life

Many divorced women find it difficult to move on with life if they did not initiate the divorce. Some women remain in denial and shock, not wanting to make decisions or be alone the rest of their lives. Some of them would rather stay in the marriage in fear of their husband instead of moving on. Sometimes they view the time spent in the marriage as a waste of their lives if they should get a divorce, and some find it difficult to see any good thing in the failed and unhappy marriage.

My concept of my marriage is that its foundation was not started on good ground; however, I am so happy for my children and the lessons I learned from being with Bert. They were good lessons and bad ones, and I am thankful for them all because I believe they have prepared me for this period of my life. I can redirect my focus, my energies, and design my life my way with the help of God. I can now live a life without regrets while I care for my children and maintain myself through the process of healing in every area. I know so many people fight for the house, furniture, cars, and money. I left the house, cars, and furniture and only took the money I had saved after I contributed my portion to our household expenses.

I have more money now than ever in my married life. I invested my money in real estate condominiums, and I'm now involved in property management that I delegated to a real estate firm.

Be True and Love Yourself

Many divorced women and men find it difficult to love themselves or others. Often they are afraid that if they let their guards down and fall in love again, this new person will hurt them. Therefore, they settle for a life of depression, withdrawal, and abandon every person and thing that meant something to them instead of having a productive relationship or growing by doing things they were not able to do in their unhappy marriage.

I began loving myself in different ways. I researched health spas and signed up to have weekly facials, massages, pedicures and manicures, hair care, and became certified for life and wellness coaching and started my health business. Eating the right organic foods with proper nutrition is important to me. I was diagnosed with a large eight-centimeter tumor that was lodged near my spine. Emergency surgery was supposed to last for three hours but was extended to over eleven. To God is the glory. I'm here to encourage others to take your health and your happiness seriously. This vessel called your body is irreplaceable, so take care of it. I now demonstrate love for my children and myself by eating and cooking healthy meals.

Rediscovering My Love

Aubrey wastes no time seeking me. All members of my thirty-five plus club have my contact information, and at the first opportunity, Aubrey contacts me. He is so pleasant on the phone. He wants to know when I can put aside some time to speak with him. We talk on the phone all night long; thank God neither of us have to work the next day. We talk so much, I fall asleep with the phone to my ear. Of course, I call him to apologize. We set up time to talk over dinner the next day, and it is as though it were only yesterday we last saw one another.

So many things are clearer to me. He tells me how he was framed, and I tell him I had been informed about it, and his case is being reopened. He tells me the lawyer had gotten in touch with him, and he was given a written apology. He mentions his lawyer informed him they had settled his case, and he shows me the check for five million dollars. He wants to know about my life and what has happened since the last time we saw each other. I ask him if he can handle what I am about to share with him. He says he never stopped loving me, and he knows that although I did get married and have children, he also knows something bad had to happen to force me to take that route.

I share everything with Aubrey as I weep throughout our conversation, especially when I tell him that my parents were included in this conspiracy with Bert. I tell Aubrey I never stopped loving him and that I felt like damaged goods and refused to marry him because of the rape, which resulted in the pregnancy of my firstborn. Aubrey tells me he heard about it and was so troubled he was not there to protect me from such horrific abuse. He says he knew my heart belonged to him and that although Bert damaged my flesh, he couldn't take my heart because it was never his.

Aubrey tells me he was involved in many relationships but couldn't marry any of the women because he always saw my face and heard my voice saying our promise. He tells me he refused to have children by any woman but me. We both weep and embrace with a connection unbelievable to the naked eye.

I don't know how long we hold onto each other, but it is as though time has stopped.

We realize time had passed, and we are the only customers left at this exclusive restaurant. I urge Aubrey we need to leave—it is past time for the restaurant to close. He tells me he owns it, and that this is a chain of restaurants local and national. Aubrey tells me he went ahead when he was released from jail and continued his education and graduated two years ago with his PhD in psychology and is in private practice. He also consults with many multimillion businesses.

Aubrey and I begin to date, and we renew our promise not to have sex until the night of our wedding. We have more fun than when we were first dating. After two months, I introduce my children to Aubrey, and incredibly, they bond in ways so strong, you would think he is their father. Martha confides in Aubrey about dating and what she should look for in a man. Aubrey shares with her the pact we made years ago about dating.

Aubrey has his own home, and many times he cooks and invites my children and me over for breakfast, lunch, and dinner. His home is so beautiful with all conveniences, but we agree we should have a home of our own. Aubrey wants to sell, but I tell him not to. Instead, he should take a tenant. I tell Aubrey the story of how my colleague helped me escape back to Guyana. I want a small wedding, and I want her as my special guest.

Our Wedding

Aubrey and I set a date for our wedding. We put together our list of guests. I do not want my parents to be in attendance. I need time, but Aubrey urges me to believe that things will work themselves out. Aubrey drops the legal case against my parents and Bert. The court is not pleased, but he says I went through enough, and he does not want me to have to relive the pain of the abuse. I drop the case of wanting to know whether my parents are indeed my birth parents. It was taking up too much of my time, and where my life is going, I have no room for bitterness or distractions.

Our wedding is held at one of Aubrey's restaurants, and our reception is held in one of the ballrooms. Everything is beyond perfect. My children are in our wedding party with Aubrey's family and some of my family and our colleagues. My father walks me down the aisle, and I believe it is the most peaceful time of my life. Aubrey weeps when my father gives him my hand. When Aubrey sees me, he can't take his eyes off me, and he whispers, "You are more beautiful now than when we met."

We exchange our wedding vows according to God's Word. It is beyond anything we have ever dreamed of. We renew our covenant to each other. Besides Bert, I have never been with another man, and here I am with my love as though we were never apart. To God is the glory.

Loving My Husband

I believe God placed Aubrey and me together, and no man or situation can pull us apart. I believe Aubrey and I were destined to be together. Aubrey fathers my children as though they are his own. Looking at Aubrey caring for them brings tears to my eyes.

After our wedding, Aubrey divides the five-million-dollar check among my three children and places it in an account for them in their names. Martha's portion is available now since she has graduated from college.

My gift to my husband Aubrey is a surprise. Three months after our wedding, I begin to feel a weird but familiar feeling. I see my doctor, unbeknownst to my husband, and am told I am pregnant. I prepare a special dinner for the family, and after the kids are settled in for the night, I slip into a negligee and tell my husband we need to talk. He says, "It must be important because your face is glowing.

You are so beautiful!"

I kiss him and whisper, "We are pregnant."

My husband looks amazed and says, "Honey, please don't joke." I take out my doctor's note and hand it to Aubrey.

With forced speech, he says, "All my life I awaited this moment to hear you are pregnant with my child."

My husband calls the doctor early the next morning and schedules an appointment for both of us to have a consultation to know what we need to be aware of in expectation of our addition to our family. My husband talks about getting a new house with more room, but I discourage him. We tell the kids when I am in my fifth month. They are so excited when they hear I am pregnant with twins, a boy and a girl. My husband wants me to quit my job soon, but I make arrangements to switch departments to launch a brand-new online program to be introduced in my district. I go back to school and complete my Online Education Innovation and Technology doctorate degree. My husband is so shocked when we prepare for my graduation with honors. With this new position, I do not have to go to an office, but can work from anywhere. God is so faithful. It is important to wait on the Lord.

Love Doesn't Hurt

The word *love* is used by so many of us for different reasons and at different times. Love means different things to different people. But do we understand what love is? I remember Bert saying "I love you," but to me, these were hollow sounds. They had no impact on my spirit when Bert said these three little words to me. Now when Aubrey says "I love you," these three little words have such an impact on my spirit, they give me goose bumps all over, from the crown of my head to the soles of my feet.

The same people who abuse women, even by men who rape or kill women, use these three little words. Now I know these three little words have lost their real meaning by being misused by so many people that they may mean different things at different times to different people. But if we look to the Word of God, we can know what the different levels of love truly mean. In the Bible in the book of 1 John 4:8 (NIV), it says, "Whoever does not love does not know God, because God is love." God's purpose is for His children to love first themselves. God wants us to also love Him and next to love our brothers and our sisters as we love God. As John 15:12 (NIV) tells us,

"My command is this: Love each other as I have loved you."

True Meaning of Love

This four-letter word *love* is so meaningful and serves different purposes. The word *love* means a strong fondness for another person we have personal ties to. Another meaning of love is a strong fascination based on one's sexual desire or lust for someone. Yet another meaning of the four-letter word *love* is based on appreciation, compassion, or shared interests that exist between two or more people. Love also means warmhearted attachment, passion, or attentiveness that someone feels for another. Love is also generous, faithful, and caring concern one may have for the good of another person.

God our Father is concerned for His children because He created us and is interested in our well-being. We should demonstrate natural affection or Storge love, or the love and affection a parent should show his child and a child for his parent. While in Philia love, the affection of friendship is divided into three types, which are the following: friendship of utility, formed without any regard to the other person. These are acquaintances or short-lived relationships, such as when people are placed in our lives based on an assignment at hand. Another Philia love is friendship of pleasure, or when we delight in others' company based on similarity of hobbies or expressions. This can be short-lived or long, based on the bonds formed. In friendships of good relationships, it is enjoyment of character and is coined true friendship because each person benefits in this friendship.

Now let's examine the Eros love or the intimate form of love. This is romantic love, such as that between my husband Aubrey and I. This love is between married couples, and it is great. We respect each other, and we are not only naked but also transparent with each other. We keep no secrets from each other, and we have no hidden agendas. We say what we mean, and we mean what we say. We protect each other and communicate with respect to each other. We demonstrate and show love to each other and to our children. We pray and enjoy family time and correct our children's behavior in love.

Aubrey and I know about our finances we had before we got married and our financial plans we have since we have been married.

We worship and are involved in ministry together, and we teach our children about tithing and demonstrate what this means.

In Agape love, divine or self-sacrificing love as explained in the Bible in the book of 1 John 4:19 (NIV), "We love because He first loved us." This kind of love is the uppermost form of love. This is the type of love God used to create us, and He continues to love us regardless of our obedience or disobedience. This love includes variances, from demonstrative to "tough" love. Again in the Bible in the book of 1 Corinthians 16:14 (NIV), it is stated to "do everything in love." Sometimes we have to do or say something to someone "for his or her own good," even if we don't want to. God's intention is for us to love each other as we love Him. But if we do not know what love means, and we do not know how to love ourselves, it is difficult for us to love ourselves the way He instructed us to love. One of our purposes is to find our way back to God's love so we may enjoy the love of others. In the Bible, the book of Proverbs 8:17 (NIV) says, "I love those who love me, and those who seek me find me." The greatest way we can love God is to praise and worship Him with our hearts, minds, and souls. God loves us so much, He delivered each of us from our own sins through the blood and sacrifice of His son Jesus Christ.

In the Bible in the book of John 3:16 (NIV), it reads, "For God so loved the world that He gave His one and only Son, that whoever believes in Him shall not perish but have eternal life."

We have to learn how to humble ourselves and become vulnerable with this understanding of a higher love and to begin to trust instead of holding on to hurt and pain. Many times we lose focus with our assignment from Abba Father, and we get into relationships that were not ordained. We then pray to ask God to fix the person when God never wanted us to be in that relationship. Sometimes we are vulnerable and want someone to love us, and they don't love themselves, and in turn, we become abused because we did not leave when we had the opportunity to. It is so vital for us to learn the things we need to do to love ourselves. I learned I first have to love me.

Loving Me for Who I Am

When I began to love myself, I gained the confidence and high selfesteem I needed. I stopped making apologies for being abused and focused on what I need to do to take better care of myself. Aubrey and I spend quality time parenting our children and as much quality time loving each other. I have met so many people who invest the bare minimum in their lives, then sit around waiting for Mr. or Ms. Right before they do anything, like learning a new skill or enjoying a career. Many of my friends and family never left the country but are instead waiting to travel when they get married, so they have no understanding of other cultures or how other parts of the world function. These people have the money but are waiting for either their husband or wife to appear before they live life! All they do is work and go home or maybe to church sometimes. I love to travel, and when I ran away from Bert, I was traveling with my children to some of the most beautiful places.

I have met so many people who tell me they are waiting on God to send their husbands or wives, but I say to them God is waiting on you. God says when a man finds a wife, he finds a good thing. Many women don't try to keep their homes clean or cook for themselves. Most of their money is spent in the drive-through at the fast-food restaurant because they don't know how to cook, and they are not trying to learn or take some culinary arts classes. Loving ourselves is shown in how we care for our homes, our finances, and ourselves. To the people who are waiting on God, God is waiting on you to decide to chase the life you deserve to live. It is your responsibility to fight for your life by first loving yourself and getting to know you in ways you have never known. Love doesn't hurt. So if you're still trying to decide whether or not love should hurt you, make a decision and give yourself permission and tell your mind you either have to love you or leave you. Period! No more vacillating between different opinions. Many people waiver between two opinions. In the Bible in the book of 1 Kings 18:21, it says, "And Elijah came unto all the people, and said, How long halt ye between two opinions? If the Lord be God, follow him: but if Baal, then follow him. And the people answered him not a word."

Women Matter

Women, the time is now for us to come into the truth about who God said we are. Women are not an afterthought.

In the Bible in the book of Genesis 1:26–27, it says, "Then God said, 'Let Us make man in Our image, according to Our likeness; let them have dominion over the fish, over the birds of the air, and over the cattle, over all the earth and over every creeping thing that creeps on the earth.' So God created man in His *own* image; in the image of God He created him; male and female He created them."

Women's spirits were created with the words of God; we are so pure, God did not touch us. God instructed man and woman by saying, "Let them have dominion over the fish of the sea, and over the fowl of the air, and over the cattle, and over all the earth, and over every creeping thing creepeth upon the earth." We were instructed by God to have dominion or authority over things, not over each other. In verse 27, it says, "So God created man in his own image, in the image of God created he him; male and female created he them."

When a man abuses a woman by raping her, burning, savaging, attacking her, prohibiting her from interacting with family and friends, and stripping her of her self-confidence and self-esteem, he is doing these things to himself.

In the Bible in the book of Genesis 2:7, it states, "And the Lord God formed man of the dust of the ground, and breathed into our nostrils His breath and man became a living soul." Genesis 2:18 also says, "And the Lord God said, 'It is not good the man should be alone; I will make him an help meet for him.'"

We women were created as a helpmeet for our husbands, not their slaves. In the Bible in the book of Genesis 2:21–23, God further stated, "And the Lord God caused a deep sleep to fall upon Adam and he slept: and he took one of his ribs, and closed up the flesh instead thereof; And the rib, which the Lord God had taken from man, made he a woman, and brought her unto the man. And Adam said, this is now bone of my bones, and flesh of my flesh: she shall be called Woman, because she was taken out of Man." God blessed both man and woman as equal bearers of His image, and we are joint recipients to rule the earth.

Motherhood

Women are unique in so many ways. Women's entire beings, including our bodies, are designed by God to undergo physical changes during fetal development and childbirth. Many women work outside and inside the home during and after pregnancy. During my pregnancy, I held a full-time job while attending college full-time. I kept up with medical appointments while continuing appointments for my hair, nails, facials, and massages. This did not stop me from making healthy meals daily and still maintaining the upkeep of my home. I worked and attended college up to my ninth month and returned to work and college after the birth of my children. My children were breastfed. I still maintained and contributed my financial responsibilities for the upkeep of my home and family. So don't think or tell me women don't matter.

Ending the Pandemic of Domestic Violence

Domestic violence was first a thought or concept in the minds and hearts of men. It manifested in its observable form in actions of physical, sexual, economical, emotional, and verbal abuse against women in relationships with individuals who are abusers. Many women are abused every second globally, and many of these women are killed. Many cultures and countries in the world ignore the horrific epidemic of domestic violence of women for one or several reasons. Sometimes it was because many people felt these women's lives didn't matter because the women were prostitutes or lowlives. But women of every ethnic background, every neighborhood, every culture, and every socioeconomic class, every country globally, every education stratum, in every business or corporation, and from every area everywhere are plagued by domestic violence.

Many women in government, even in ministry as pastors, suffer from the silent pandemic of domestic violence, and they are so afraid and ashamed to let anyone know. Some may die a silent, horrifying death, and these women never live to tell their story. Some give up on life because they feel their lives don't matter because their abusers are in high-power jobs or are respected in the community. These men continue to afflict the abused and beaten-down women, and these women come to believe no one would protect them if they should speak up.

Too many people wrongly lament a woman can just leave if she chooses. These people are ignorant to the fact that the most dangerous time for a woman to leave is when she is being abused. I know because I was one of those women.

To Thine Own Self Be True

So many women don't know they are significant. So many women compare themselves to idealized fantasy versions of other women's physical attributes, size, skin color, and physical physique, and other women's weight. Too many women base their worth on their careers, education, skills, experiences, cultures, socioeconomic standing, neighborhoods, or a million other external, superficial traits. Other women base their significance on the groups they join, such as women's rights groups, or on how their family, friends, or men see them.

These women would continue to be abused, misunderstood, manipulated, and misinterpreted by others. I refused to be abused any longer when I stumbled upon the reality of what makes me different from another.

I gained wisdom when I recognized I was different from others. No one looks like me, talks like me, is compassionate like me, loves like me, or is anointed by God like me. So I refused to allow Bert or anyone else to abuse me. I stopped the comparison game because it was seeking the wrong answer. We are not valuable because of how we compare; we are valuable because God uniquely and perfectly made us. Men and women must now transform their minds with God's perspectives of who they are according to the purpose of God's will for their lives. They must study the Word of God and apply it to their lives, not by what man calls them or writes about them or by their religiosity or their cultures or even their churches.

Women—Who Are You?

I would hear the women in my neighborhood whispering to each other or sometimes having a conversation about a woman who was being beaten. Many of the conversations would reflect the idea that it serves this woman right to get a beating because she should know her man's meal needs to be cooked and ready when he gets home. These gossiping women would continue by saying they know a workingman must have his food as soon as he gets home. This workingman is a good man and takes care of his family by paying the bills and keeping a roof over their heads. Sometimes these women would distance themselves from the woman who was beaten and would continue to say it was her fault and she deserved it. These women would conclude a good woman would make sure her man is cared for before the children.

When the battered woman is able to rejoin the neighborhood women, she would never complain about the abuse. Instead, she would claim she knows her man must love her because if he didn't, he wouldn't beat her. The battered woman would reassure the other women and her family members that everything was great between her and her man and their relationship was better now than it ever was. The battered woman never acknowledged the beatings as abuse, only that she made a mistake by not performing her duties as a woman, and she would do better moving forward. After the beating was over and things appeared to be settled in the household, the older women in the community would take the battered woman and educate her on the ways to make her man happy. Part of the counsel to the abused woman was that if nothing else were done, be certain his meals are cooked and ready to be served on time.

God's People Are Abused

Although both men and women are abused and can be abusers, the majority of the batterers are men abusing women. This book addresses abuse against women. I have survived abuse and domestic violence and will share with you how we all can collaborate to eliminate abuse and domestic violence globally. Domestic violence is the result of learned behaviors that exist against women in every country in the world. Much domestic violence occurs in homes, organizations, families, and in communities, and many times these abuses are unreported. Any person who uses violence of physical abuse, sexual abuse, verbal abuse, psychological abuse, and economical abuse to control another person suffers from low self-esteem and confidence, confusion of identity, and doesn't know his self-worth. The abuser refuses to accept responsibility for the abuse and blames the abuse by justifying his horrific actions. Women often return to their abusers. I was one of them because I lacked faith. Bert could have killed me. I humbled myself and learned God's Word for my life, and some of my messages are found at Gumroad.

Tell Pharaoh to Let My People Go

Escape from domestic violence reminds me so strongly of the time in the Holy Bible when God sent Moses to Pharaoh. Moses was sent to Pharaoh to tell him to let God's people go, and after many signs of plagues, God's people were set free. However, as God was using Moses to take them to the Promised Land, these people began to complain and compare their journey to when they were living in Pharaoh's country and enjoyed melons, leeks, and garlic. The Israelites had fallen in love with their abuser, Pharaoh, and once situations became challenging after they fled, they wanted to return to Pharaoh.

Bert tried to sway me with temptations of our beautiful home and amenities and how wonderful it would be for me to return there. I admit, I struggled with the idea of whether I should return to him. I must say, for a moment, I was lured by my memories of hazy hindsight, but God reminded me that when He closes a door, I should not try to open it.

Why Are the Roles of Men and Women Misunderstood?

Many past and current issues surrounding domestic violence stem throughout the nations from the misunderstanding of the role of a man and a woman in the homes, workplace, and in society. These issues globally impact the different cultures of the world and are due to the contradictory ideas of what the role of a man and woman is. Many countries in the world place a lesser value on women than on men. This lesser value affects women in many areas of their lives, including our careers, self-esteem, confidence, ability to balance our lives, performance of our God-given purpose, our skills, and our overall potential. Women have always been told about the things they can do, should do, and can't do. Women have always been told to stay in their place.

I'm not sure where this place is though. Prior to graduating with my bachelor's degree, I asked one of my professors for a reference to graduate school. His response to me was, "Now that you have your bachelor's degree, you need to be a mother to your children." He went on to say he believed my bachelor's degree was good enough for me and that I didn't need further education. Funny, I did not ask for his opinion. Needless to say, he never did give me a reference.

Globally, women have always been told what our role should be and what our rights are. Women are always told we deserve what happens to us, including domestic violence. We are told and continually reminded that we are weak. We provoke the violence. We lead our abusers on. We are our mates' servants. On jobs, oftentimes the women are looked upon to prepare the coffee and clean up after the men. Women are paid less for performing the same jobs as men. Women are treated as inferior to men. We are men's personal property, servants of men. Women are treated as second-class citizens.

Globally, due to the impact of domestic violence on women, we have suffered, and some women have been killed while others die spiritual deaths. Still, some women have died because they did not understand that the longer unproductive people are allowed in their lives, the longer the defeated devil is empowered. During the years of abuse, the relationship was unstable due to role confusions. As I was struggling with coordinating my responsibilities as a wife and mother while maintaining my career, I was struggling to balance work and career—meeting my family's needs, the responsibilities of our home, and ensuring money was available for the maintenance of our needs, while my then-husband was displaying role confusion of what he thought my responsibility was. At the same time, he was unsure of what his responsibilities as the head of the household were. His confusion overlapped into his role, which he thought was only to contribute 50 percent of his income toward the family budget, period. As per my ex-husband, according to his upbringing, a man's job did not include any household responsibility or nurturing his family or using verbal communication. He said nothing was wrong with him throwing his clothes on the ground because it was my responsibility to pick up after him.

Many women don't understand their purpose or function or know their assignment in their life. Domestic violence causes many women to abort their visions, dreams, abilities, and desires, and this results in women accepting things, situations, ideas, and people who negatively impact their lives. Many women suffer from domestic violence and accept it as part of their lifestyle.

I find that due to the confusion and misunderstanding of a woman's role worldwide, these negative ideas of the expectation of a women have compounded the issues, which are now widespread, impacting women all over the world as they continue to be abused in relationships and to continue to suffer domestic violence. A woman's role is so misconstrued, many men feel that instead of her being their helpmeet, the woman is in the men's life primarily to make him happy. I need to enlighten all women, including myself, that the day the men are unhappy, they will blame us for this unhappiness. Many men don't know their purpose, and like women, they too are looking for their happiness in the external environment, such as in their relationships, through a woman. When they feel frustrated or disappointed—unhappy—abuse and domestic violence occur. When a man doesn't understand the purpose of the woman he shares his life with, it is a breeding ground for discontent and possible domestic violence. It is key to read and understand the Bible.

Women Have Rights

I have never been in favor of women's rights or women's groups representing or demanding women's rights because I understand my God-given rights. Many of my friends are not in agreement, and they feel I'm odd because I don't advocate for these groups. However, I would be wrong to believe I have no inherent rights and need to ask for rights. Every woman must understand God gave us these rights. They were given to us in the beginning when God created us. Women must grasp this and apply it to every thought. If not, some women will continue to allow men to feel they have to give us permission to have rights because they have the power and we have none.

I remember as a teenager, I never fit in because I felt no one had the right to dictate my God-given rights. Though I didn't quite understand this, for some reason, I was never in agreement and was always vocal with my opinion. I have always advocated my significance is what I tell myself it is, and not what someone else tells me. I grew up in church, but I was never in agreement with the things I heard and saw in reference to how women were poorly treated. Many of the married male leaders at my church were having affairs with women in their congregation and preaching about the word of God concerning divorce and relationships. The same male church leaders were also abusing their wives and thought nothing of it. Many of the members in the ministry were aware of the abuse and the infidelity of their church leaders but were silent about it. I believe silence is a form of agreement. When we are silent about things that are wrong, we too will be held responsible because indeed we are our brother's and sister's keepers.

Some countries have made efforts to protect the rights and respect of women, while other countries are not making enough of an effort to protect their women's rights. Because the different cultures globally have different ideas about women's roles and their identities, which can be contradictory, our self-worth, self-esteem, and our identity have decreased and continue to be diminished.

Prophetic Shape Shifter

We may not all be ordained as Prophets of God, but we all must prophesy God's truth in and over our lives. God's truth is found in His Word or His Will for our lives. Whatever someone finds himself or herself experiencing, he or she must go into the Bible and look for scriptures that talk about the situation. Invite the Holy Spirit, our teacher, to teach us the revelation and truth about our situation and only speak that truth. Yes, admit the facts of the situation, but believe with God all things are possible, including healing in your situation. Only if we believe in a miracle of healing from abuse can we prophesy a miracle in this area.

According to Our Faith

Miracles go where our faith develops expectations. You can't think you would be healed. Instead, you have to use your voice and speak your thoughts into words for your healing from abuse to begin. Your words would create jurisdiction on earth. Continue to raise your belief for healing, and your faith will be increased. God said it is according to your faith, not His faith, or our prayers, or how effective or long we pray. Your faith is in the deep recesses of your spirit, and when you speak life over your situations, only your faith the size of a mustard seed would become activated by your own words. God created us all. So many people are destroyed from the lack of knowledge, and I see so many people going astray by things and people. I was once this person because I did not know who I was. Women, whatsoever you name your situation, God will honor you. Be careful what you call yourself or allow others to call you.

Stop Prophesying Your Disasters

The Kingdom of God cometh not by observation, and the time is now for us to demonstrate the talents that God has blessed us with. We must take our rightful places in God's Kingdom and stop waiting for changes, but become the change agents. When people get something, they say this is the will of God. When people don't get what they want, they say this was not God's will. God gives each of us a mission for our lives, and this is more important than our jobs and businesses. Be careful of the opportunities you dive into, and put them before God to know whether He ordains them for you.

God Is a Just God

It's our time to stand still and see the salvation of the Lord. This is visualization, which God will work for us this day. Women who are abused will be justified and vindicated by God. So, abusers, unless you repent and turn from your wicked ways, know you will reap the same seeds of abuse you have planted. Abused women will see the salvation of God. We must also repent and forgive the abusers so God will forgive us our trespasses. God is our judge, Jehovah Shaphat. We must become true worshipers by redeeming time with God by getting into His Word and asking the Holy Spirit to give us the discernment of each word for our lives.

Creation and Formation

In the first book of the Bible, Genesis 1:1–3 says, "In the beginning God created the heaven and the earth. And the earth was without form, and void; and darkness was upon the face of the deep. And the Spirit of God moved upon the face of the waters. And God said, Let there be light: and there was light." We must be intentional about what we say and what we speak over our lives and situations. God created the heavens and the earth, but it was only when God spoke the words aloud that the Holy Spirit moved upon those words God said to bring these things into manifestation. Therefore, only when we say something out loud, either life or death, do these words go into the universe and take up earthly jurisdiction.

God created His sons and daughters by His Word. The hands of God out of the dirt formed Adam's physical body, but God's Word created Adam's spirit. In the Bible in the book of Genesis 2:19, it shows, "And out of the ground the Lord God formed every beast of the field, and every fowl of the air; and brought them unto Adam to see what he would call them: and whatsoever Adam called every living creature, that was the name thereof."

Creation is spiritual, but formation is physical and is made by things already existing. We must be careful of our negative thoughts because things are created first in the spiritual realm, then they take up earthly jurisdiction or show up in the earthly realm. Whatever is seen in the earthly realm was first created in the spiritual realm. It's time for us to clean up any negative thoughts. We have to assess the quality of our thoughts.

How to Transform Our Minds

Women, we have to change our thoughts by arising from our present condition of abuse or where we are to what we wish our life to be.

We have to follow God's instructions to Abram in the book of Genesis 13:14–15: "And the Lord said unto Abram, after Lot was separated from him, Lift up now thine eyes, and look from the place where thou art northward, and southward, and eastward, and westward: For all the land which thou seest, to thee will I give it, and to thy seed for ever."

To solve our problems, we must first understand the Gospel and its two parts. The first part is about the person of Jesus Christ, who creates our peace in preparation for eternity, and the second part teaches us how to activate the principles of Jesus Christ to create our prosperity and prepare us to live on the earth. Our transformation comes when we solve the problems of the horrific abuse we have sustained and, in turn, educate other women and men, including our sons, to eradicate abusive thoughts and behaviors. We must now shift our thoughts from the conditions of hatred and envy, bitterness, unforgiveness, strife, and malice to loving ourselves and demonstrating love to others.

God said He would forgive us our debts as we forgive our debtors. To fight the loneliness, we must see ourselves with healthy companions and having friends. Our help cometh from the Lord, but to get help, we have to lift up our eyes. We must come up higher because too many times, women want to hold on to their abuse and wreck their spirit with unforgiveness by looking down at their situations instead of activating the help God has for them.

We Must Get This!

Our physical bodies are our homes, and this is the only home God has given us. God wants us to think like this. So when we get up to move, our home moves with us because the house we live in is not our homes. Our bodies are crucial, and we need them to function on earth. Jesus Christ needed a body, and He was born of a woman. Demons and angels can't function on earth without a physical body. God needs our bodies, so He goes through our bodies to function on earth. When men lose this physical body, they lose the right to function on earth. When men violate a woman's body, a spiritual discord is unleashed, and this is not acceptable to God.

God's Service

God is not looking for people to have a special place, but to take our temples to turn our whole house into the presence of God. Your life should be called God's altar, and you should worship God where His altar resides. Wherever I go is where I carry this altar of God, and it goes with me. Our bodies are the temples of the Holy Spirit. Jesus told the woman, "The day is coming, and now is when you don't have to go to Jerusalem nor this mountain to worship God."

Who are the true worshipers? True worshipers dwell with the Holy Spirit and live with the Holy Spirit in the same temple.

The Temple of God

Abusers seek to destroy the temple of the Holy Spirit. You don't have to go to the mountain or Jerusalem to pray or to a church to pray. My temple, my physical body, goes where I go. I don't need to set a space aside in a closet to pray because I am a true worshiper, and true worshipers carry God's temple wherever they go. Bring the temple of God to wherever you go, and sanctify and take over where God sends you. But true worshipers, Jesus said this worship is done in the temple of the Holy Spirit. True worshipers respond from their spirits. It is vital to have continuous fellowship with the Holy Spirit because there are so many things God wants to tell us, and too many times, we get busy with things that bring us no discernment.

Fellowship with the Holy Spirit

True worship allows you to hear and see things to come. Activate your spirit by speaking in tongues. Singing in tongues gets to our emotions, but this is not deep enough. True worship is fellowship with the Holy Spirit in humble submission, and you bow in the spirit before the Holy Spirit. You become conscious of the Holy Spirit and lay everything before the Holy Spirit because you become intertwined with the Holy Spirit. Everything is before God, and God fills you and me and strengthens us and gives us the confidence and boldness as our faith is increased. You and I receive power because the Holy Spirit is in us, and the anointing of the Holy Spirit is running through every fiber of our being. This is the ministry of the Holy Spirit.

Recommendations to Globally Eliminate Abuse of Women

I realize I had many wrong ideas and feelings, and to become who God said I am, I had to first correct my thoughts and begin to have right thinking. I have rejected the facts that had me accepting the things society and others said about me, and I have now moved into the truth of who God says I am. When women begin to think correct thoughts, have right ideas, only the correct thoughts can replace the wrong thoughts, and the right thinking will replace the wrong thinking. Abuse occurs in these aspects: educational, employment, verbal, physical, and mental/psychological, sexual, gender, financial, spiritual, and medical. Where does domestic violence fit in?

Domestic violence first exists as a thought and a feeling in the minds and hearts of men and women, and it is manifested in its visible form in the actions of physical, sexual, verbal, emotional, and economical abuse. There can be relationships of both heterosexual and homosexual individuals who are abusers and their victims. Any person who uses violence of physical abuse, sexual abuse, verbal abuse, psychological abuse, and economical abuse to control another person suffers from low self-esteem. The abuser may refuse to accept responsibility for the abuse and may believe the abuse is justified. Often the batterer will try to minimize the abusive behavior or blame the victim for causing it. The tendency to use abuse as a control tactic sometimes may be aggravated by the use of drugs and alcohol, and many times, domestic violence is transferred from one generation to another. Children growing up in homes of domestic violence many times in their adult lives may display the abusive behaviors they have witnessed.

Some abusers attribute alcohol and substance abuse as the reason for abusing an intimate partner; however, overcoming a drug or alcohol problem does not always end the abusive behavior. Why do I say this? Many times after a restraining order is filed, and someone is sentenced to serve time in jail, and the person is released from jail, the abuse does not stop. Neither does justifying the abuse by using alcohol as the reason is acceptable. Some professionals may feel batterers can overcome abusive behaviors through the appropriate treatments, such as counseling, therapy, medication for anger management, and separation from their abusive environment, separation from their substance abuse, or by leaving the partner they have abused.

However, as a psychotherapist for over twenty years, I believe that although those treatments are important, the abuser must decide to stop—to be released from being an abuser. And that is just the first step. The ultimate truth is that the only way a man will wholly eliminate abusing a woman is when he comes into the truth and realization of who God says he is because the truth shall make him free. As he finds his purpose in life, he will change his mind of abusing women because he will now have a free mind. God said, "Let this mind be in you which was also in Christ Jesus" (Phil. 2:5, NKJV).

I believe as men make a decision in their hearts and minds to forgive themselves for their bitterness and anger, they can be free in their minds and hearts to create their own lifestyle by using energy to live their passion and purpose, which is to create. It is only at this level where men are able to change nations globally, by first educating themselves and their immediate family about the truth of who God says they are. When men forgive, they get control back into their own lives. These same men will be able to speak God's truth about who a man is into other men's lives who are abusing women globally, and this will result in many free men.

The Truth about Who We Are

God created both men and women in His image. "Then God said, 'Let us make mankind in our image, in our likeness, so that they may rule over the fish in the sea and the birds in the sky, over the livestock and all the wild animals, and over all the creatures that move along the ground'" (Gen. 1:26). God created both men and women equal, but with different functions and different purposes. When God created man, God drew man out of himself. God is a Spirit: and they that worship Him must worship Him in spirit and in truth" (John 4: 24); therefore, man is also spirit. The creation of man is spirit. However, when God made Adam and Eve, this process was quite different from when God created man. Because to make something means something is formed from some kind of substance or material that is available. It is like making a cake. The ingredients have to be there to be put together to make the cake (and I am certified in culinary arts). Therefore, God first created man by drawing man out of His spirit. God made male and female from substances God had there.

After God formed Adam, God formed Eve. God called male and female *man* after He created us because God was referring to our spirit He put in us when He created us.

Healing in the Mind

Healing always first begins in the mind. Therefore, a sick or unhealthy person should always begin to see themselves in a healthy or desired light in their mind. They should visualize the desired goal or state of health in their mind on a consistent basis. They must learn to see themselves as they desire to be when they visualize, and this desire can materialize in the physical form. I had to forgive myself for making the mistakes I did and ask for forgiveness for the things that were done to me in my past. It was only then I began to love myself.

Man Lacks God's Knowledge

When men abuse women, they are also abusing themselves because they are abusing the man within the female. In Genesis 1:26–28, it says, "And God said, 'Let us make man in our image, after our likeness: and let them have dominion over the fish of the sea, and over the fowl of the air, and over the cattle, and over all the earth, and over every creeping thing that creepeth upon the earth.

So God created man in his own image, in the image of God created he him; male and female created he them. And God blessed them, and God said unto them, Be fruitful, and multiply, and replenish the earth, and subdue it: and have dominion over the fish of the sea, and over the fowl of the air, and over every living thing that moveth upon the earth.'"

God was referring to the spirit man, which refers to both the male and female because the spirit man exists in both the male and the female. God said the spirit man, male and female, should both have dominion, and God blessed them. A lover is a giver, and the giving comes from the spirit of the man.

Become a Giver

God is love, and God created our spirit man, which is male and female, in love. When you love, you give. God so loved us, He gave His only begotten son. When one demonstrates true giving without an ulterior motive, one becomes a lover. God says to give thanks for everything. Men, instead of abusing your wife, become a giver—this would give you the faith to stop violating yourself. When men abuse women, men are abusing themselves because God's plans and purposes are being rejected. Many of us are not studying and understanding God's purpose for our lives; therefore, we continue to depend upon our pastors, cultures, family, and our limited experiences to teach us about God's purpose for our lives. Misunderstandings of generations are passed down to us and now have resulted in communication and relationship problems between men and women and have spread to the nations in the world in the form of domestic violence.

The Right Leadership

When the right leadership is in your life, you will serve God. When Israel had wrong leadership, they served their gods, and God called them stiff necks. When men have fathers who are poor leaders, they become poor leaders in their homes. Be careful who is speaking in your life and from whom you're getting counsel from. You must know who is supposed to shepherd you so your faith can be strengthened. You must have the right counsel and stay with it. You must hear the voice of the Holy Spirit speaking through your leader.

Stop connecting to people God rejected. The wrong leadership— whether at work, in your home, or your church—loves to elevate itself. These leaders reject God's anointed and counseling given by God's chosen vessels. Sometimes the vessels are the wives of pastors. Many husbands have parents but no father as leaders to lead them. God did not send a husband to attack his wife and to destroy his home. Dome as the head or leader is equivalent to the head of the family. The anointing flows from the dome and down. When a woman is abused and violated by her husband, a violation occurs to the dome, and violence enters the head along with wrong thinking. With this violation, giving stops. When domestic violence stops and right thinking returns to the dome or head, everyone begins to give, and love flows. With this giving, the anointing flows and frees the minds of the abusers, and this spreads from country to country.

Study to Show Yourself Approved

We live in a microwave world, and many people want everything right away. Few people invest in their spiritual lives. So many people want to be entertained and refuse to invest in attending spiritual conferences, workshops, or biblical teaching. Until I began to ask the Holy Spirit for help and to study the Word of God and to enrich my spiritual life, I allowed myself to be spiritually abused because the extent of the Word of God did not go beyond what the pastor said in church. My purpose or what God's Word said about me was unclear to me. I accepted abuse in my marriage because that is what I saw in my family, and they never left their husbands who abused them. God is not doing for us the things He knows we need to do for ourselves. Until I began to seek God first and His righteousness and renew my mind, I experienced years of abuse and sustained severe consequences. God said we must worship Him in spirit and in truth. We need to find God's purpose for our lives and to understand how we should function in harmony with ourselves, each other, and with the people who have abused us.

God said He wills everything for our good; therefore, we must switch our focus to be great students of the Holy Spirit so we can begin to use what we call the trials and tribulations and have them work toward our good to complement each other. It is only at this point in our lives that we will come into harmony with each other and the universe. God wants us to be in good health and prosper as our souls prosper. So many of God's people experience ill health and think that if God wants to heal, He would. They have misunderstood. His Word states in the Bible that my faith and your faith have made us whole. God gave us different talents and watches over us to see what we do with the talent to either increase us when we use the talents to fulfill His instructions or to take the talent from us. What have you done with your talents that you were given? This is how I have documented my talents.

My Journey to Spiritual Restoration

As I began my journey of healing and transformation, the Holy Spirit instructed me to write a chapter in *The Queens' Legacy*. I got an email that they were looking for people who wanted to be featured as authors to write a chapter in an upcoming book. I read the email, but I was embarrassed to let anyone know I was raped and abused. The Holy Spirit instructed me to answer this call. I wasn't happy at all. I did answer and did what was instructed, but all the while I was praying my submission would be rejected. It was accepted, and I began to write it contrary to the Holy Spirit's instructions. It disappeared from my computer. I cried, and the Holy Spirit instructed me to follow His directions, and I did. I became brave enough to attend a conference that would give me the strategies to become a motivational speaker. I panicked and thought of running away from this conference when I was given an assignment to speak in front of the audience, but I did not want to feel like a failure. I went ahead and shared my reason for wanting to be the voice of abused women who are unwilling to advocate for themselves, and the *Who You Be* CD was created.

Les Brown told me I had a book inside me. I laughed. But his voice became a nag in my spirit. Another person asked me for the name of the book I was yet to write, and the Holy Spirit said *My Journey to Spiritual Restoration.* So my book was birthed (buy it on Amazon).

Who Are You?

I would like to share something with you, and I would like to ask you, who are you? Who do you think you are? We define ourselves by how society defines us, how our families see us. So when I ask you, "Who are you?", you probably cannot answer without thinking of society, by defining ourselves as a doctor, a teacher, a pastor's wife, a mother, a homemaker. I am here to talk to the other you within you.

Listen, life at times throws us all kinds of curveballs. At three months of age, a cousin who did not like me because of the color of my skin poisoned me. I was abused and molested. I was sick for many years. I suffered academically and socially. At a young age, I decided I had to take the authority of my life and fight for it, and I realized every day will be a fight. I have to determine who I am, and you have to determine who you are. Let's go through the journey. You have hidden seeds of greatness within you. You are going to go through struggles in life. Many people look at life as the harbor. We go to college as society tells us to, do all the right things, get a good education, get a good job, get married, buy a house, and we think this is life. But it is not life because it does not determine who you are. Until you begin to make a commitment and begin to walk in your true potential, you will never know who you are.

Many of us have been faced with challenges: abuse, marital issues, drugs, death in the family, sickness, and relationship issues. When I was getting my master's degree, I lost two siblings. I became angry; I realized I had to take care of my life. I couldn't leave it to anyone else. I stopped myself and said, *The things I wouldn't tolerate in my life, I won't allow.* As a single parent, I did not want my children to be abused, and sometimes, life issues cause us stress. We use drugs to numb the pain, and we become the abusers. Sometimes we even abuse ourselves. But we don't have to. You don't have to accept abuse in your life. You are awesome, powerful, unstoppable, and you have to make a choice.

Use the Tests as Testimonies

Give testimonies of the goodness of God. I thank God daily that I'm alive and in my right mind. So many people didn't make it for so many reasons, but I'm here, and I'm in the best season of my life. When I assess my life and its difficulties—what we refer to as trials and tribulations—I realize God was preparing me all along for His assignments. I had to change my mind and ask the Holy Spirit to transform my thoughts to be more appreciative and to understand God's assignment for my life. I had to see the goodness in my tribulations as is written in Hebrews 13:5: "Let your conversation be without covetousness; and be content with such things as ye have: for he hath said, I will never leave thee, nor forsake thee." I had to agree with God's plan for my life. When God says these things would work together for my good, I had to listen.

I began to get involved in volunteering my time, knowledge, skills, education, and experiences to improve the lives of women and men in the workplace, in the education systems, in mental health, in the classrooms, in colleges, in ministry, and in the communities.

Restoration of God's Anointing

God's restoration is powerful, and only He could have restored me to Himself. It feels so wonderful to know and feel I am being restored to my original position in the image and after the likeness of God, of having dominion over every situation in my life, as is written in Genesis 1:26–27. I am so thankful to God for restoring me back to the image He created of me with His image and with the new things He's doing in my life. With His new thing comes the new anointing of the Holy Spirit, and for this, I'm so grateful. I know what it is like to feel connected with God and to have a relationship with Him as a true worshiper, worshiping God in spirit and in truth, worshiping God wherever He sends me.

God's Spiritual Restoration for His Church

God is calling His church back to Himself. In the Bible in the book of Acts 2:17, it tells us, "And it shall come to pass in the last days, saith God, I will pour out of my Spirit upon all flesh: and your sons and your daughters shall prophesy, and your young men shall see visions, and your old men shall dream dreams."

God continues to say in Joel 2:25, "And I will restore to you the years the locust hath eaten, the cankerworm, and the caterpillar, and the palmerworm, my great army which I sent among you." Remember, restoration means the creation of something that surpasses the original. This restoration represents to the church the type of love Jesus manifested during His ministry on earth. Restoration also means the manifestation of God's unlimited power through His church. It will occur when the gifts of the Holy Spirit flow through God's people and toil without limitations and restrictions under the direction of the Holy Spirit. The church will be able to get to a place of maturity through the manifestation marked by the Holy Spirit of the gifts and ministries established in the body of Christ as these works to the divine nature of Christ. The time is now for the church of God to be converted into a holy and consecrated place that will, in turn, convert God's people back to Himself, and the world will see the glory of God's final restoration.

God Is Restoring His People

God is calling us to prayer and fasting for our spiritual restoration and to guide us back to Him. In the Bible, God said in the book of Joel 1:14, "Sanctify ye a fast, call a solemn assembly, gather the elders and all the inhabitants of the land into the house of the Lord your God, and cry unto the Lord." God is calling us to a fast, and we must be obedient.

Fasting and Prayer

When my life was filled with turmoil, I didn't understand fasting or what it meant. I began to seek the Lord. I went before God, and I was instructed to learn about fasting. I researched fasting and the different types of fasting, and I fasted for more than 110 days. I read my Bible from cover to cover and prayed throughout the day. I saw the miracles of God, and my entire life began to change for the better in remarkable ways. I began to seek God and His kingdom first. I began to trust and depend on God, and for the first time in my life, I felt good depending on and trusting God. No longer did I feel burdened by trying to figure out how things were going to work out in my life and in my family's life, and this felt great—so freeing.

God's people must seek Him first and by first sanctifying a fast collectively among their family and in their households and pray and ask the Holy Spirit to guide them. Families should not rely on their pastors only because so many pastors are not praying or fasting or seeking God first. So many church members are sitting in so many of these churches, big and small, and these members are ill and disconnected from their creator God. God is doing a new thing for His people who are obedient, faithful, and available by following His instructions. After this, God's people who are called by His name shall be restored from spiritual death with spiritual life. But we will not only receive a new type and quality of life, but we shall also grow in it and through the Holy Spirit. God will continue to perfect the work begun with our salvation.

God's people have the anointing of God flowing through us, and when God's heart touches our hearts, this anointing will also flow through our hearts, the anointing of the Holy Spirit. This anointing will flow as love from our hearts to the hearts of all the believers when we connect with them, restoring them to receive God's touch through us. This anointing is for God's service through us to do the work our Father God placed us here to start and to complete at each of our assignments. It is not for us to be used, to abuse, to rule over people, or to promote ourselves, thinking it is about us—like we have arrived. God anoints His chosen people who love Him and put Him first over their own assignments. It is vital for us to open our hearts to love God's people so He can allow His anointing to flow from us to those whom God designated to receive it. The anointing of the Holy Spirit is given through God's people to demonstrate God's power and love.

God's Anointing on My Life

The right location and relationship are keys to my anointing and to my faith. Don't allow anyone to limit your faith and limit your anointing. The years I was married to Bert weakened and drained my anointing. My spirit life was stifled. I made all kinds of wrong decisions because my anointing was weak, and these wrong decisions got me into so much trouble. During this time, I was no longer walking in divine favor or grace.

Maintain God's Anointing

Whatsoever you do, don't you ever lose God's anointing because you will have a great problem along with weak and limited faith and poor judgment. God's glory was taken from King Saul, and God replaced it with an evil spirit. Your thoughts will be negative with lots of limitations. Be careful who you have speaking in your life and who you are taking counsel from. The defeated devil comes to steal, kill, and destroy, and many times, people have devilish behaviors, and we keep them in our lives while justifying this relationship. God said to resist the devil, and he will flee from you. Resist people with devilish behaviors.

When God wants to bless us, He places a person in our life to flow this blessing through. When the devil wants to destroy us, he also sends a person in your life, and your life becomes hell and impairs your health and wellness. God said money answers all things (Eccles. 10:19), so stop settling and allowing people to handicap you by hindering your money movement, or else you'll have no answers to anything. Negative people would drain God's anointing out of you and sabotage your faith. Protect God's anointing in and on your life. No one can survive if only negative things, bad news, and negative people surround you.

Bert was not satisfied with what God was doing in my life. Bert tried to drain my faith in God with his negative energy and his controlling and abusive behaviors. My parents tried to limit my faith and destroy my anointing when they forced me to marry the rapist Bert.

My Spiritual Restoration

God is continuously restoring His anointing in and on my life, and I do guard it. No longer will I allow anyone to limit my faith or relationship with God. Now God leads me, and my spirit is free. My faith is strengthened daily, free to worship and praise God. God removed me to restore me. God continues to move in my life in miraculous ways. Like the four lepers, God wants me to move. God said when He moves, I should move, and God continues to cover me under His cloud. I refuse to miss God's plan and will for my life. My faith is strengthened, and I am happy and excited because I know God is with me. I became so bold and strong when I allowed God to restore me unto Himself.

Living in French Guiana limited me because I couldn't speak the language, and the culture was so different from mine, along with the isolation from everything I knew, so I had to get out of there. So many people stay in places God rejected them from, and they are falling ill, but they are too stubborn to leave because they feel they have to be a good Christian by enduring, but they lack God's wisdom.

God's Spiritual Restoration

I remember I had lots of challenges when it came to being humble. However, my journey and experiences going through the years of trials and tribulations with dangerous experiences caused by domestic violence have taught me to be humble. At my lowest, I went before God to learn how to pray, and I began to pray and to volunteer to intercede for God's people. Therefore, I became an intercessor, which helps me remain humble before God. I developed such a strong desire for God's people. My spiritual restoration began when God told me to write *My Journey to Spiritual Restoration*, and this was the turning point in my spiritual life and relationship with Abba Father. Don't allow your flesh to stay in any situation that is not congruent with God's anointing in and on your life. You must make a decision to be obedient to God. I did, therefore, choose to follow God's instructions to complete this book, *Love Me or Leave Me: A Contemporary Memoir*. To God is the glory.

Ms. Fraser survived many harrowing experiences. She was poisoned at three months old, raped at four years old, and abused by a partner with a weapon. God healed her from an eight-centimeter tumor spread on her spine. A high school student physically assaulted her; she suffered from five dislocated discs in her upper and lower back and two dislocated discs in her neck.

Ms. Fraser is a licensed school social worker, a psychotherapist for over twenty-five years, a special educator, a certified speaker, a certified life coach, and a health and wellness coach. Ms. Fraser received the Award for Designing the Creative Work Environment.

Ms. Fraser served on the Domestic Violence Advisory Board and the Beginning Teachers Leadership Network. Ms. Fraser is certified by the Women's Commission Speaker Bureau and at UNC Love Speaks Out, and she serves at many events.

Ms. Fraser is a sought-after speaker and has made several appearances on television, radio stations, women's groups, churches, and businesses and has spoken on several topics that bring insights to many people.

Follow me–
Website www.gurmayfraser.com

Facebook–
https://www.facebook.com/profile.php?id=100069727068451

Instagram–
https://www.instagram.com/gurmayfraserofficialpage/

Twitter–
https://twitter.com/gurmay

LinkedIn–
https://www.linkedin.com/in/gurmayfraser/